# D R E A M S

### O F

# D E S T I N Y

Green Acre
Bahá'í School

AMIR BADIEI

# DREAMS

## OF

# DESTINY

IN THE BÁBÍ AND BAHÁ'Í FAITHS

Baháʼí
PUBLISHING
Wilmette, Illinois

Bahá'í Publishing
401 Greenleaf Avenue, Wilmette, Illinois 60091-2844
Copyright © 2013 by the National Spiritual Assembly of the Bahá'ís of
the United States

16   15   14   13        4   3   2   1

Library of Congress Cataloging-in-Publication Data

Badiei, Amir.
  Dreams of destiny / Amir Badiei.
  pages cm
  Includes bibliographical references and index.
  ISBN 978-1-61851-045-7 (alk. paper)
  1. Dreams—Religious aspects—Bahai Faith. I. Title.
  BL65.D67B33 2013
  297.9'342—dc23
  2013019340

Cover design by Andrew Johnson
Book design by Patrick Falso

# DEDICATION

This book is dedicated to the infants of the Bahá'í families who are languishing with their mothers under the most deplorable conditions of Simnan prison in Iran. These tender souls are in prison solely because they were born to Bahá'í parents. I dream of a day in which the whole human race will live in a world free of religious and all other forms of prejudice, this baneful social disease.

# ACKNOWLEDGMENTS

I wish to express my sincere gratitude to Mrs. Dorothy Pedersen, a member of the Bahá'í community of Salem, Oregon for devoting much of her precious time to the proofreading of the manuscript and for making constructive suggestions for its improvement.

I would also like to thank Mr. Christopher Martin, an editor at the Bahá'í Publishing Trust, who generously spent his time in editing and in assisting me in the preparation of the manuscript for publication.

To my daughter, Soha Badiei, I extend my gratitude for her continuous encouragement and her ever-present support.

# CONTENTS

# INTRODUCTION TO THE BAHÁ'Í FAITH

During the nineteenth century, many religious scholars all over the world were expecting the appearance of their Promised One. Some students of Christianity had come to the conclusion, based on the Bible's prophecies, that the return of Christ would take place during the 1840s. There were also some Muslim theologians who were expecting the appearance of their "Lord of the Age" at about the same time. In particular, there were two prominent theologians who were proclaiming the imminent return of the "Lord of the Age" and were preparing their students for the Advent of the promised Qá'im. The first of the two was Shaykh Aḥmad Al-Aḥsá'í, who was followed by his successor, Siyyid Kázim-i-Rashtí, who died in December, 1843.

In May, 1844, a young merchant of Shíráz* named Siyyid 'Alí-Muḥammad, declared His new mission and assumed the title of the Báb. He announced to the people that He had been sent by God to usher in a new age and to prepare humanity for the imminent appearance of another Messenger greater than Himself.

The force of the Báb's character and utterance attracted many people to Him and soon He had a great many followers who became known as the

---

* A city in the southwest of Iran, and the capital of Fars province.

Bábís. The first eighteen individuals who accepted His claim became known as the Letters of the Living. The Báb Himself and His followers came under immediate attack from the religious and governmental authorities in Iran. Almost all the Letters of the Living and thousands of His followers were fiercely and savagely persecuted and eventually killed. In a few occasions, some groups of these hunted and desperate Bábís banded together and rose in self-defense against the forces of aggression. The Báb Himself was publicly executed in the city of Tabriz* in July 1850.

Bahá'ís believe that the Báb was an independent Messenger of God, Who initiated a new religion called the Bábí Faith. At the same time, He was the Forerunner of the great Messenger to come, Bahá'u'lláh, much the same as John the Baptist who foretold the coming of Christ.

Bahá'u'lláh was, at first, one of the followers of the Báb and publicly championed His Cause. His given name was Mírzá Ḥusayn 'Alí, and He belonged to an eminent and wealthy family of Tihrán, the capital city of Iran. Like other Bábís, He was also persecuted and eventually imprisoned under the most appalling conditions. After nearly four months, the king of Iran agreed to let Bahá'u'lláh leave the prison but decreed that He must be banished from Iran.

Bahá'u'lláh's first place of exile was Baghdád, Iraq. After living in Iraq for some ten years, He was banished, for a second time, to Istanbul. Just before leaving Baghdád, Bahá'u'lláh declared Himself to be that long-awaited Messenger of God promised by the Báb. After this announcement, the new religion became known as the Bahá'í Faith. Bahá'ís believe that God, throughout history, has revealed Himself to mankind through a number of Divine Teachers, Whose teachings guide and educate us. These teachings are the basis for the advancement of human society. Bahá'u'lláh is the latest in a line of Messengers of God that includes Abraham, Moses, Buddha, Christ, and Muḥammad.

---

* A city located in the northwest part of Iran, and the capital of East Azerbaijan Province.

After a short stay in Istanbul, Bahá'u'lláh was banished to Adrianople,* where he resided for a few years. It was in this city that Bahá'u'lláh proclaimed His message publicly by writing a series of letters to the then temporal and spiritual leaders of the world. In these letters, He informed their recipients of the advent of His Revelation and summoned them to international unity, arbitration, and universal peace.

His next and final banishment was to 'Akká,† which occurred in August 1868. He spent the last twenty-four years of His life in and around this city which, at that time, was a penal colony and one of the most desolate cities in the world. He passed away in Bahji, a suburb of 'Akká, in 1892 at the age of seventy-five. By then He had spent forty years of His life as a prisoner and an exile.

Before leaving this world, Bahá'u'lláh appointed His eldest son 'Abdu'l-Bahá as the head of the Bahá'í Faith and the authorized interpreter of His teachings. 'Abdu'l-Bahá's ministry lasted for twenty-nine years until His passing in 1921. In His Will, He designated His eldest grandson, Shoghi Effendi, as His successor. He was referred to by the Bahá'ís as the Guardian of the Bahá'í Faith, a title which was conferred upon him by 'Abdu'l-Bahá. The Guardian's ministry continued until his death in 1957, which marked the end of a period during which the Faith was being guided by a single individual. The center of authority and the highest governing body for the Bahá'í Faith today is the Universal House of Justice. It is composed of nine members who are elected every five years by members of more than 180 national-level governing councils worldwide known as National Spiritual Assemblies.

During His lifetime, Bahá'u'lláh wrote many volumes of books, through which He enunciated His principles, outlined His teachings, and answered diverse questions that came to Him from His followers and others. Bahá'ís consider His writings to be the revealed Word of God, and they are now translated into more than eight hundred languages.

---

* Its modern name is Edirne. It is a city in the northwest of Turkey near the border with Greece.

† 'Akká or Acre is a city in northern Israel at the northern extremity of Haifa Bay.

In His writings, Bahá'u'lláh also established the institutions of His Faith and the pattern of its future organization. The Bahá'í Faith has no clergy, and its affairs are administered by governing councils that operate on local, national, and international levels.

The basic goal of the Bahá'í Faith is to bring about the unification of the entire world. Bahá'u'lláh taught us that there is one God, that there is only one human race, and that the basis of all the divine religions is one. He has stated, "Revile ye not one another. We, verily, have come to unite and weld together all that dwell on earth." He has also stated, "The earth is but one country and mankind its citizens."

Further, Bahá'u'lláh has given us a set of principles and a social structure to facilitate bringing about the unity of the diverse peoples of the world. Some of these principals are:

1. The independent investigation of truth
2. That religion must be the cause of unity
3. That religion must be in accord with science and reason
4. The elimination of prejudice of all kind
5. The equality of men and women
6. Universal access to education
7. The adoption of a universal auxiliary language
8. Spiritual solutions to economic problems
9. Universal peace upheld by a world government.

To enumerate all the principles is beyond the scope of this short introduction. Mention must be made, however, of the importance Bahá'u'lláh has placed on two other principles: justice and consultation. He calls justice "the best beloved of all things" in the sight of God. He also singles out consultation as the key for settling disputes and for developing plans and policies for the common good.

Today, the Bahá'í teachings and principles are put to practice throughout the world by millions who come from different racial, cultural, ethnic, and economic backgrounds. They all believe that the message of the Bahá'í Faith is uniquely relevant to the problems and concerns facing humanity in today's world. Bahá'u'lláh states, "The All-Knowing Physician hath His finger on the pulse of mankind. He perceiveth the disease, and prescribeth, in His unerring wisdom, the remedy. Every age hath its own problem and every soul its particular aspiration. The remedy the world needeth in its present-day afflictions can never be the same as that which a subsequent age may require" (Bahá'u'lláh, *Gleanings from the Writings of Bahá'u'lláh*, no. 106.1).

# INTRODUCTION

"Among these [individuals who awaited the advent of the Promised One in Karbilá] was Ṭáhirih,* fasting by day, practicing religious disciplines, and spending the night in vigils, and chanting prayers. One night when it was getting along toward dawn she laid her head on her pillow, lost all awareness of this earthly life, and dreamed a dream; in her vision a youth, a Siyyid, wearing a black cloak and a green turban, appeared to her in the heavens; he was standing in the air, reciting verses and praying with his hands upraised. At once, she memorized one of those verses, and wrote it down in her notebook when she awoke. After the Báb had declared His mission, and His first book, 'The Best of Stories,' was circulated, Ṭáhirih was reading a section of the text one day, and she came upon that same verse, which she had noted down from the dream. Instantly offering thanks, she fell to her knees and bowed her forehead to the ground, convinced that the Báb's message was truth."[1]

The foregoing is the story of Ṭáhirih's acceptance of the Báb's claim as told by 'Abdu'l-Bahá.† The Báb's first book, "The Best of Stories," (Aḥsa-nu'l-Qiṣaṣ) which is mentioned above, is the *Qayyum'l-Asma'* or "The Com-

---

* The first woman to accept the Báb as the Manifestation of God. She was one of the Báb's first eighteen followers who became known as the Letters of the Living.

† One of the central figures of the Baháʼí Faith and the son of its Founder, Baháʼuʼlláh. See Dream #63.

mentary on the Súrih of Joseph," which was regarded by the early Bábís as the Qur'án of the Bábí dispensation. Since the Qur'án refers to the story of Joseph as the best of stories, "We tell thee the best of stories, in inspiring thee with this Qurán,"[2] its commentary, written by the Báb, was also known as "The Best of Stories."

Whatever the truth behind the literal account of Joseph's earthly life, as related in the Bible and the Qur'án, its spiritual and symbolic significance has been of paramount interest to countless religious scholars. In essence, it represents the prototype, the illustrative pattern, of the life of the Perfect Man, or of any of the Manifestations of God. Bahá'u'lláh, for example, identifying Himself with Joseph, states, "Again Thou didst cast Me into the prison-cell of the ungodly, for no reason except that I was moved to whisper into the ears of the well-favored denizens of Thy Kingdom an intimation of the vision with which Thou hadst, through Thy knowledge, inspired Me, and revealed to Me its meaning through the potency of Thy might."[3] This divine and enduring story has run, like a common thread, through the writings and expositions of Judaism, Christianity, Islám, the Bábí religion, and the Bahá'í Faith. Besides, the story of Joseph, with its numerous interpretations and commentaries, has permeated and greatly enriched mankind's literature throughout the world. *Joseph and his Brothers*, for example, is a four-part epic novel written over a period of sixteen years and is one of the largest and most significant literary works of its author, Thomas Mann, the German novelist.

The story of Joseph, the last patriarch mentioned in the Book of Genesis, first appears in the Old Testament. It is an interesting account of Joseph's life that runs for fourteen chapters, and it is one of the longest and most absorbing stories in the Bible. In Christianity, it has been taken to be a paradigm foreshadowing the trials and the triumphs of Jesus Christ's earthly and spiritual life. Some Christian scholars have listed numerous parallels between the story of Joseph and that of Jesus Christ. Subsequently, the story was retold in Islám in the authoritative and the most enchanting language of revelation, taking up one entire súrih (chapter) of the Qur'án. This twelfth súrih of the Qur'án is permanently and intimately associated with the opening scene of the Báb's declaration to Mullá Ḥusayn on the eve of May 22, 1844.

Addressing him, the Báb said, "'Now is the time to reveal the commentary on the Súrih of Joseph.'"[4] Bahá'u'lláh has characterized this commentary as ". . . the first, the greatest, and mightiest of all books . . ." in the Bábí Dispensation.[5] The Guardian tells us that the fundamental purpose of this commentary was "to forecast what the true Joseph (Bahá'u'lláh) would, in a succeeding Dispensation, endure at the hands of one who was at once His arch-enemy and blood brother."[6]

In the writings of Bahá'u'lláh and 'Abdu'l-Bahá, we find frequent references to the story of Joseph. In The Four Valleys, for example, Bahá'u'lláh says, "Methinks at this moment, I catch the fragrance of His garment blowing from the Egypt of Bahá; verily He seemeth near at hand, though men may think Him far away."[7]

Joseph is portrayed in both the Old Testament and the Qur'án as a man with a pure heart, high integrity, forgiveness, wisdom, and knowledge. In the latter, it is stated, "And when he had attained his maturity, We gave him wisdom and knowledge: and thus do We reward those who do good."[8] God had also favored him with the talent and the skill to interpret dreams. For this, Joseph expresses his gratitude to the Almighty by saying, "O my Lord! Thou hast indeed bestowed on me some power, and taught me something of the interpretation of dreams and events . . ."[9] Joseph's knowledge and understanding of dreams played a critical role in the course of his life. He was first released from the prison and, subsequently, established on the seat of power by accurately interpreting the dreams of his two prison-mates and those of the pharaoh. He also had his own fateful and prophetic dream, which he related to his father, Jacob: "O my father! I did see eleven stars and the sun and the moon: I saw them prostrate themselves to me!"[10] Much later, when his parents and his eleven brothers fell down in prostration before him in Egypt, Joseph said, "O father! this is the fulfillment of my vision of old! Allah hath made it come true!"[11] Hence, the story of Joseph becomes the story of a dream, its epiphany, its progression, and its fulfillment. Saeidi has written that "The realization of the dream in the realm of phenomena is the historical revelation of the invisible and eternal divine truth,"[12]—that is, God's progressive revelation.

Joseph's course of life, profoundly influenced by his dream and his ability to interpret dreams, had a significant impact on the ensuing history of the Israelites. Through his guidance and influence, they first migrated to the land of Egypt, settled there and, subsequently, grew to a great multitude. Their increased number alarmed the Egyptians, who adopted an oppressive attitude towards them. This eventually forced the Israelites to lead a life of servitude and slavery and culminated in the appearance of a great Manifestation of God, Moses, among them. It was Moses who led the oppressed Israelites in their exodus out of Egypt, taking the bones of Joseph, the dream interpreter, with them.

Dreams have played a significant role in almost all the religions and cultures of the world. Some people have thought of dreams as a link between man and the spiritual world, the hallowed realm. As stated by Bulkeley, "Nearly all the world's religions share the belief that some dreams are true revelations of the Divine, bringing people into direct contact with some kind of trans-personal being, force, or reality."[13] This same idea is expressed in the book of Job: "For God may speak in one way, or in another, yet man does not perceive it. In a dream, in a vision of the night, when deep sleep falleth upon men, in slumbering upon the bed; Then he openeth the ears of men, and sealeth their instruction, That he may withdraw man from his purpose, and hide pride from man."[14]

A cursory survey of religious writings indicates a distinct possibility of the concurrence of religion and dream from the beginning of time. There are many references to dreams in the early Hindu writings. The book of Genesis, probably the oldest Jewish literature, contains several significant dreams of the patriarchs. We have already made references to those dreams that were related to the story of Joseph. Before His birth, Zoroaster's parents dreamed that they would have a child who would change the world. According to Shoghi Effendi,* Zoroaster was awakened to His mission by a succession of seven visions.[15] The Buddhists believe that a dream by Queen Maya,

---

* He was the grandson of 'Abdu'l-Bahá, the Guardian and appointed head of the Bahá'í Faith from 1921 until his passing in 1957. See Dream #73.

the mother of Buddha, was the herald of His conception in her womb. In the Gospel of Mathew we encounter dream as a vehicle for revelation. Four times, Joseph receives divine communications through dreams. In the Qur'án, dreams are mentioned mainly in connection with the stories of the past prophets, such as the dreams associated with the story of Joseph and that of Abraham's concerning the sacrifice of His son. And finally, in Bábí and Bahá'í literature, we find numerous dreams, many of which will be related on the following pages of this book.

Dream has often been regarded as a phenomenon that can foretell a future event. Bahá'u'lláh states, "Behold how the thing which thou hast seen in thy dream is, after a considerable lapse of time, fully realized."[16] 'Abdu'l-Bahá says, "It often happens that a man in a state of wakefulness has not been able to accomplish the solution of a problem, and when he goes to sleep, he will reach that solution in a dream."[17] History traces the roots of a great number of discoveries to dreams. The discovery of the chemical transmission of nerve impulses by Otto Loewi, a German-born physiologist, for example, is a case in point. It was his dream that guided him in this discovery for which he won the Nobel Prize for medicine in 1936. And according to Einstein, his theory of relativity first came to him in a dream.

In the writings of Bahá'u'lláh, the Báb, and 'Abdu'l-Bahá, the phenomenon of dreaming is often cited as a proof for the existence and immortality of the human soul. 'Abdu'l-Baha has made a statement to the effect that God has created dream to make the people believe in the existence of other worlds and in man's perpetual growth.[18] In his well-known poem, "The Dream," Lord Byron says, dreams "look like heralds of eternity."[19]

To elucidate the existence of the human spirit and its independence from his physical entity, the Prophets of God, philosophers and thinkers have all alluded to the phenomenon of dreaming. James Lewis writes, "It has also been postulated that at least one of the sources of the idea of a soul distinct from the body is dreams. During dreams, one has the experience of traveling to other realms, interacting with people, and doing various things; simultaneously, the physical body remains confined in bed. While the dream realm is shadowy and surreal, it nevertheless feels like a place apart from the world of everyday experience. Therefore, it is not unreasonable to speculate that during dreams the conscious self somehow separates from the body. If we add to this the common experience of meeting departed friends and relatives in dreams, it is no giant step to conclude that the same 'soul' that separates from the body during dreams also survives the death of the body. If this hypothesis is correct, then dreams also contribute to the idea of a soul as it has traditionally been formulated in most world religions."[20]

On this very subject, Bahá'u'lláh writes, ". . . Had the world in which thou didst find thyself in thy dream been identical with the world in which thou livest, it would have been necessary for the event occurring in that dream to have transpired in this world at the very moment of its occurrence. Were it so, you yourself would have borne witness unto it. This being not the case, however, it must necessarily follow that the world in which thou livest is different and apart from that which thou hast experienced in thy dream. This latter world hath neither beginning nor end. It would be true if thou wert to contend that this same world is, as decreed by the All-Glorious and Almighty God, within thy proper self and is wrapped up within thee. It would equally be true to maintain that thy spirit, having transcended the limitations of sleep and having stripped itself of all earthly attachment, hath, by the act of God, been made to traverse a realm which lieth hidden in the innermost reality of this world. Verily I say, the creation of God embraceth worlds besides this world, and creatures apart from these creatures."[21] In the Seven Valleys, Bahá'u'lláh says, ". . . Luqmán,* who had drunk from the wellspring of wisdom and tasted of the waters of mercy, in proving to his son Nathan the planes of resurrection and death, advanced the dream as an evidence and an example."[22]

'Abdu'l-Bahá has further expanded on this theme and said, ". . . But in the world of dreams the soul sees when the eyes are closed. The man is seemingly dead, lies there as dead; the ears do not hear, yet he hears. The body lies there, but he—that is, the soul—travels, sees, observes. All the instruments

---

* He was a wise and saintly man. Chapter 31 of the Qur'án is named after him. His words of wisdom and advise to his son Nathan are found in this chapter of the Qur'án.

of the body are inactive, all the functions seemingly useless. Notwithstanding this, there is an immediate and vivid perception by the soul. Exhilaration is experienced. The soul journeys, perceives, senses."[23]

According to 'Abdu'l-Bahá, there are three kinds of dreams. One kind is a spiritual (precognitive) dream, whatever transpires in the dream the same occurs in the real world. 'Abdu'l-Bahá says that this kind of dream is like the morning light; it needs no explanation or interpretation. But this kind of dream is quite rare among people. The second kind is a dream that requires interpretation. Here an individual with aimless thoughts may, in his dream, have a spiritual excursion. To extract the meaning of that spiritual sojourn and to expound its significance, the dream must be correctly interpreted. To illustrate this, 'Abdu'l-Bahá gives the following example. If a yellow piece of fabric is dyed blue, the result would be a green piece of fabric. The blue color will appear only after the yellow color of the fabric is removed. This demonstrates how interpretation works; the intrusive elements are identified and eliminated so that the true message of the dream is realized. The third kind is a confused dream which has neither an interpretation nor a true message. It is the product of a fanciful and delusive mind.[24]

The Báb has commented that one must act according to the substance/message of a dream if it is in conformity with the teachings of the Cause of God. And if it is not, it must be disregarded.[25] In a letter written on his behalf, the Guardian stated, ". . . That truth is often imported through dreams no one who is familiar with history, especially religious history, can doubt. At the same time dreams and vision are always colored and influenced more or less by the mind of the dreamer and we must beware of attaching too much importance to them. The purer and more free from prejudice and desire our hearts and minds become, the more likely is it that our dreams will convey reliable truth, but if we have strong prejudices, personal likings and aversions, bad feelings or evil motives, these will warp and distort any inspirational impression that comes to us. . . . In many cases dreams have been the means of bringing people to the truth or of confirming them in the Faith. We must strive to become pure in heart and 'free from all save God.' Then our dreams as well as our waking thoughts will become pure and true.

We should test impressions we get through dreams, visions or inspirations, by comparing them with the revealed Word and seeing whether they are in full harmony therewith."[26]

The significance of dreams and the events associated with them in the Bábí and the Bahá'í revelations can hardly be overemphasized. Both Bahá'u'lláh and the Báb received Their first intimations of Their sublime missions through weighty and soul-stirring dreams.* Shoghi Effendi clearly states that it was in consequence of a potent dream that Bahá'u'lláh was invested with the power and sovereign authority associated with His Divine mission.[27] And it was through dreams that the truth of Their missions was subsequently imported into the bosom of the great many of Their followers and supporters. In reality, the course of the history of the Bahá'í Faith and the lives of many of its adherents have been profoundly affected by dreams. A number of these dreams, some of which are of immense significance, are cited in the following pages of this book. Also recounted here are some other stories of lighter nature that are merely interesting.

An attempt has been made to present these dreams chronologically, that is, through the order of their appearance in the successive unfoldment of the events in the Bábí and Bahá'í history, and not necessarily in the order in which the dreams were dreamed.

Many of the dreams are preceded by an introductory section to familiarize the reader with the personalities, circumstances, timing, or the historical events associated with each one of these dreams. Gaining insight into these spiritual dreams, which 'Abdu'l-Bahá likens to the "morning light," awakens one to the receptivity and the potentialities latent in any heart that is pure and free from all save God. In addition, these dreams, in conjunction with their introductory write-ups, will provide the reader with a refresher course in some selective and dramatic segments of Bábí-Bahá'í history.

---

* Dreams #9 and #33.

# 1

Before the conquest of Iran by the Arabs, Estakhr was the biggest and the most important city in the area which is known today as the province of Fars (Pars).* After the fall of Iran and during the rule of 'Abdu'l-Malik Ibn Marwan, Muḥammad Ibn Yusuf Thaqafi was appointed as the governor of this area.† Under the influence of the following dream, this governor undertook the building of the city of S͟híráz, some thirty to forty miles south of Estakhr. By the passage of time, S͟híráz became more important and the inhabitants of Estakhr transferred their residence to the newly established city.

One night the governor had a dream in which he saw that a number of angels descended from the heavens and prostrated themselves on the site where the city of S͟híráz stands today. In his dream, the governor heard them saying, "The people of nobility will appear on this location which, in the future, will become the milieu of the holy ones, the refuge for the poor, and the fountainhead of knowledge, wisdom and purity. The travelers from the unseen dominions of God will replenish their supply at this place." In his dream, the governor drew a line around the area which was intensely illuminated. The following day, he proceeded to that locality and recognized the site, which appeared to him as bright as it was in his dream. This increased his confidence and, subsequently, he directed the planners and the builders to start their work on the erection of the city. Meanwhile, and according to the custom of the day, the governor consulted some astronomers and astrologists, who forecasted felicity and blessedness associated with this enterprise.[1]

---

* A province in southern Iran.
† The Umayyad Caliph, who ruled from 685 to 705 A.D.

# 2

Before the Báb's declaration in 1844, there were two Muslim theologians, one after the other, who heralded His advent. The first one was Shaykh Aḥmad-i-Ahsá'í, the founder of the Shaykhí school in Shí'ah Islám. The second one, Siyyid Kázim-i-Rashtí, was Shaykh Aḥmad's student and his successor. He died on December 31, 1843 a few months before the Báb's declaration. In the Kitáb-i-Íqán, Bahá'u'lláh refers to these two forerunners of the Báb as "twin resplendent lights." The early followers of the Báb were mostly of the Shaykhí school and the former students of Siyyid Kázim. When he was young and studying theology, Shaykh Aḥmad had a dream which he described as follows:

> One night, during my studying years, I had a dream in which I saw a young man of about twenty-five years of age. He came over and sat by me. Turning his face to me, he opened the book which he had with him and explained the meaning of the following two verses in the Qur'án, "Who hath created, and further, given order and proportion. Who hath ordained laws. And granted guidance; . . ."* He explained, in essence, that God created the primordial matter in every created thing and perfected its form according to what it was meant to be. Then He decreed the means necessary for every created thing and guided it to the paths of good and evil (beneficial or harmful circumstances for every kind). Then I woke up and found my soul to be liberated from the cares of this world and all that it contains. Also, I became reluctant to pursue my bookish studies any further. I kept my association with diverse people but did not tell anyone about my dream. Although I was bodily present among the people, my spirit and reality were miles and miles away.[2]

---

* Qur'án 87:2–3.

# 3

Siyyid Kázim, in his book entitled Dalílu'l-Mutahayyirín, writes: "Our master, (Shaykh Aḥmad), one night saw the Imám Hasan,* upon Him may the blessing of God rest! His Holiness put in the Shaykh's mouth His blessed tongue. From the adorable saliva of His Holiness he drew forth the sciences and the assistance of God. To the taste it was sweeter even than honey, more perfumed than musk. It was also quite warm. When he came to himself and wakened from his dream, he inwardly radiated the light of divine contemplation; his soul overflowed with the blessings of God and became entirely severed from everything save God." His faith, his trust in God and his resignation to the Will of the Most High grew apace.[3]

---

* The oldest grandson of Muḥammad and the second Imám in Shí'ah Islám.

# 4

One night in a dream it was signified to him (Siyyid Kázim) by one of the illustrious progenitors* of the buried saint† that he should put himself under the spiritual guidance of <u>Sh</u>aykh Aḥmad-i-Aḥsá'í, who was at this time residing at Yazd. He accordingly proceeded thither and enrolled himself amongst the disciples of <u>Sh</u>aykh Aḥmad, in whose doctrine he attained such eminence that on the <u>Sh</u>aykh's death he was unanimously recognized as the leader of the <u>Sh</u>aykhí school.[4]

---

* Fatima, the daughter of Muḥammad, is mentioned as the progenitor who appeared to the Siyyid in his dream.

† Siyyid Kázim was then in Ardibil (a city in northwestern Iran) near the tomb of a descendant of the seventh Imám of <u>Sh</u>í'ah Islám, Imám Musa Al-Kázim.

# 5

Every year, in the month of Dhi'l-Qa'dih,* the Siyyid would proceed from Karbilá to Kázimaynᵗ in order to visit the shrines of the Imáms. He would return to Karbilá in time to visit, on the day of 'Arafih,‡ the shrine of the Imám Ḥusayn.§ In that year, the last year of his life, he, faithful to his custom, departed from Karbilá in the first days of the month of Dhi'l-Qa'dih, in the year 1259 A.H.,** accompanied by a number of his companions and friends. On the fourth day of that month he arrived at the Masjid-i-Barátá, situated on the highway between Baghdád and Kázimayn, in time to offer up his noonday prayer. He bade the Muadhin summon the faithful to gather and pray. Standing beneath the shade of a palm which faced the masjid, he joined the congregation, and had just concluded his devotions when an Arab suddenly appeared, approached the Siyyid, and embraced him. "Three days ago," he said, "I was shepherding my flock in this adjoining pasture, when sleep suddenly fell upon me. In my dream I saw Muḥammad, the Apostle of God, who addressed me in these words: 'Give ear, O shepherd, to My words, and treasure them within your heart. For these words of Mine are the trust of God which I commit to your keeping. If you be faithful to them, great will be your reward. If you neglect them, grievous retribution will befall you. Hear Me; this is the trust with which I charge you: Stay within the precincts of the Masjid-i-Barátá. On the third day after this dream, a scion

---

* The eleventh month in the Islámic lunar calendar.

ᵗ A town about three miles from Baghdád where the tombs of the two Kázims, Imám Músá Kázim and Imám Muḥammad-Taqí, the seventh and the ninth Imám respectively, are located.

‡ In Islám, a very important day of Hajj when multitudes of pilgrims gather in the Plain of 'Arafih and pray all together.

§ The second grandson of Muḥammad and the third Imám in Shí'ah Islám. His shrine is in Karbilá where He was martyred in 680 A.D.

** November 23–December 23, 1843 A.D.

of My house, Siyyid Kázim by name, will, accompanied by his friends and companions, alight, at the hour of noon, beneath the shadow of the palm in the vicinity of the masjid. There he will offer his prayer. As soon as your eyes fall upon him, seek his presence and convey to him My loving greetings. Tell him, from Me: "Rejoice, for the hour of your departure is at hand. When you shall have performed your visits in Kázimayn and shall have returned to Karbilá, there, three days after your return, on the day of 'Arafih, you will wing your flight to Me. Soon after shall He who is the Truth be made manifest. Then shall the world be illuminated by the light of His face."'" A smile wreathed the countenance of Siyyid Kázim upon the completion of the description of the dream related by that shepherd. He said: "Of the truth of the dream which you have dreamt there is no doubt." His companions were sorely grieved. Turning to them, he said: "Is not your love for me for the sake of that true One whose advent we all await? Would you not wish me to die, that the promised One may be revealed?" . . . This strange event was noised abroad. It brought sadness to the heart of the true lovers of Siyyid Kázim. To these he, with infinite tenderness and joy, addressed words of cheer and comfort. He calmed their troubled hearts, fortified their faith, and inflamed their zeal. With dignity and calm he completed his pilgrimage and returned to Karbilá. The very day of his arrival he fell ill, and was confined to bed. . . . On the day of 'Arafih, in the year 1259 A.H.,* at the ripe age of sixty, Siyyid Kázim, in accordance with the vision of that lowly shepherd, bade farewell to this world, leaving behind him a band of earnest and devoted disciples who, purged of all worldly desire, set out in quest of their promised Beloved.[5]

---

* December 31, 1843 A.D.

# 6

On the eve of May 22, 1844, in S͟híráz, Persia, a young man, Siyyid 'Alí-Muḥammad, declared Himself as a Messenger of God come to usher in a new prophetic cycle. He took for Himself the title of *the Báb* and announced the imminent appearance of Bahá'u'lláh, the redeemer of mankind, awaited by all the peoples of the world. The title *Báb* means "the Gate." Although Himself the bearer of an independent revelation from God, the Báb declared that His purpose was to prepare mankind for the advent of Bahá'u'lláh. With this announcement, the Báb inaugurated the Bábí dispensation, and those who believed in Him and followed Him became known as the Bábís.

When the Báb was a small child, He had a dream which He related to His family: "Last night, I dreamt that a large balance was suspended in mid-air in the vast space. His Holiness Imám Ja'far-i-Sadiq* was positioned on one of the plates and because of His weight, the plate was resting on ground while the other plate was suspended in the air. An invisible Hand lifted Me and placed Me on the empty plate. My plate was now heavier than the other and I came to the ground and the first plate went to the air."[6]

---

\* The sixth Imám in S͟hí'ah Islám.

# 7

The Báb and His wife were not widely separated in age. The house of Ḥájí Mírzá Siyyid 'Alí, the maternal uncle of the Báb—who became His guardian after the death of His father, and the house of Mírzá 'Alí, the father of Khadíjih Bagum (the Bab's wife), adjoined each other; and so the Báb and Khadíjih Bagum were neighbors and playmates in their childhood. Mírzá Siyyid Hasan (the Great Afnan* of future years), a brother of Khadíjih Bagum, was about the same age. Whenever the children of the two households came together to play, usually Siyyid 'Alí-Muḥammad (the Báb) chose not to join in their games, although He occasionally did, and was always kind and considerate.

Years later, when Siyyid 'Alí-Muḥammad had gone to Bushihr (Bushire), Khadíjih Bagum had a vivid dream in which she saw her young Cousin in a verdant plain, with flowers in profusion, facing towards the Qiblih (Mecca) in an attitude of prayer. He wore a "labbadih"† on which Qur'ánic verses were embroidered with threads of gold. His face was radiant. She related that dream to her mother, and to the mother and grandmother of Siyyid 'Alí-Muḥammad. They assured her that it was her Cousin's assiduous attendance to His prayers which had vouchsafed her that splendorous vision. At this time Siyyid 'Alí-Muḥammad could not have been more than sixteen years old.[7]

---

* *Afnan* refers to the male relatives of the Báb.
† A long outer coat worn by men.

# 8

Munirih Khánum,* the wife of ‘Abdu’l-Bahá, has related the following account which she heard from the wife of the Báb (Khadíjih Bagum):

One night, I dreamt that Fatimih [the daughter of the Prophet] had come to our house, to ask for my hand. My sisters and I went to her presence with great joy and eagerness. She rose up and kissed me on my forehead. In my dream, I felt that she had approved of me. In the morning, I got up very elated, but modesty stopped me telling anyone of my dream. The same day, in the afternoon, the mother of that Blessed Being [the Báb] came to our house. My sister and myself went to meet her, and exactly as I had seen in my dream she rose up and, embracing me, kissed me on my forehead. When she had gone, I was told by my elder sister that she had come to ask for my hand. I said: "How fortunate I am," and then, I related my dream of the previous night . . .

---

* See Dream #49.

# 9

In *God Passes By*, the Guardian tells us that the Báb found Himself the recipient of God's outpouring grace after He awoke from a dream in which "He approached the bleeding head of the Imám Ḥusayn" and quaffed the blood that dripped from his lacerated throat.*

In one of His writings during His first year of ministry, the Báb Himself has made the following statement:

> The spirit of prayer which animates My soul is the direct consequence of a dream which I had in the year before the declaration of My Mission. In My vision I saw the head of the Imám Husayn, the Siyyidu'-sh-Shuhadá, which was hanging upon a tree. Drops of blood dripped profusely from His lacerated throat. With feelings of unsurpassed delight, I approached that tree and, stretching forth My hands, gathered a few drops of that sacred blood, and drank them devoutly. When I awoke, I felt that the Spirit of God had permeated and taken possession of My soul. My heart was thrilled with the joy of His Divine presence, and the mysteries of His Revelation were unfolded before My eyes in all their glory.[9]

---

* Shoghi Effendi, *God Passes By*, p. 144.

# 10

In one of His writings, the Báb refers to a dream which He had about two years after His declaration. In this dream, He saw many books that were in His presence. He opened one of them and found a folded paper in which there was some dust from the grave of the Imám Ḥusayn. As He unfolded the paper, He found a Tablet on which were some Persian writings in red ink. There was, at the end of the Tablet, a seal that was as brilliant as a star. Upon the seal was engraved the name of the Promised One, Mihdí, and the invocation, "I entrust My Cause into the Almighty's care." The writing of the Tablet was confirming the station of the Báb as the Promised One. He then proceeds with the elucidation of the inner meaning of the words on the Tablet which, in essence, discloses His own appearance on Mount Sinai. At the end, He points out that the true meaning of all the words could not be divulged because of the fear from the pharaohs and the pharaoh-like people of the time.[10]

# 11

The following is a brief description of another dream related by the Báb.

The Báb saw in His dream that there was a grave in the middle of a house in which He used to live. Upon the grave was a mausoleum. While He was approaching the grave, He saw Imám Muḥammad al-Javád* emerge from it in the utmost beauty. The Báb recognized the Imám and greeted him. Then the Imám took some candies from his pocket and gave them to the Báb. He took the candies and ate them all. After describing His dream, the Báb states that from the blessing of the Imám's gift He became very happy, and His heart became dilated."[11]

---

* The ninth Imám of Shí'ah Islám, known also as Imám Muḥammad-Taqí.

# 12

Mullá Yúsuf-i-Ardibílí was one of the Letters of the Living.* He was noted for his learning, his enthusiasm, and eloquence. In the Kitáb-i-Íqán, Bahá'u'lláh mentions his name among the illumined divines, the men of consummate learning, and the doctors of mature wisdom who had accepted the Báb's claim. After the death of Siyyid Kázim, Mullá Yúsuf went to Shíráz in search of the Promised One. At a later date, he explained his reason for traveling to Shíráz: "During the earthly life of Siyyid Kázim, I kept vigil for forty days in the mosque of Kúfih.† On the fortieth day a shepherd came to the mosque, related his dream to me and wanted its interpretation. He said that in his dream, he saw a Sun rising over the horizon of Shíráz and illumined the whole world. I took this dream to be a guiding message to me and I, therefore, decided to proceed to Shíráz."

Mullá Yúsuf-i-Ardibílí participated in the defense of the Fort of Shaykh Tabarsí‡ and was one of the martyrs in that historic event.¹²

---

\* See Dream #15.

† Seclusion and keeping vigil in certain mosques were, and still are, practiced by Muslims all over the world. To the Shí'ah Muslims the mosque at Kúfih is of special significance. Kúfih was the seat of Caliphate during the ministry of Imám 'Alí and it was in the same city that He was martyred.

‡ See dream #23.

# 13

Ṭáhirih was the only woman among the Letters of the Living and the only one who, without seeing the Báb, gave Him her allegiance as the result of a dream she had. She was born to a family of high ranking Islamic clerics in Iran. In her early years, she had acquired much religious knowledge from her father and other members of her family. One day, by chance, she discovered some books written by the leaders of the Shaykhí school, Shaykh Aḥmad and Siyyid Káẓim. Their writings were quite appealing to her and she began corresponding with Siyyid Káẓim who was residing in Karbilá. In order to study under his tutelage, she secured permission to visit the shrines of the Imáms in Karbilá and Najaf. Siyyid Káẓim had, however, died just ten days before her arrival in Karbilá. His widow allowed the deeply saddened Ṭáhirih to reside in her house and to have access to Siyyid Káẓim's writings. It was in this house in Karbilá where she had her significant dream.

This dream, as told by 'Abdu'l-Bahá, was cited in the introduction to this book. The following account of the same dream is from *The Dawn-Breakers*: "She (Ṭáhirih) joined the companions of the departed leader, and spent her time in prayer and meditation, eagerly expecting the appearance of Him whose advent Siyyid Káẓim had foretold. While in that city (Karbilá), she dreamed a dream. A youth, a Siyyid, wearing a black cloak and a green turban, appeared to her in the heavens, who with upraised hands was reciting certain verses, one of which she noted down in her book. She awoke from her dream greatly impressed by her strange experience. When, later on, a copy of the "Aḥsanu'l-Qiṣaṣ," the Báb's commentary on the Súrih of Joseph, reached her, she, to her intense delight, discovered that same verse which she had heard in her dream in that book. That discovery assured her of the truth of the Message which the Author of that work had proclaimed. She herself undertook the translation of the "Aḥsanu'l-Qiṣaṣ" into Persian, and exerted the utmost effort for its spread and interpretation."[13]

# 14

Edward Granville Browne, an eminent British Orientalist, described Ṭáhirih in these words: "The appearance of such a woman as Qurratu'l-'Ayn* is in any country and any age a rare phenomenon, but in such a country as Persia it is a prodigy—nay, almost a miracle. Alike in virtue of her marvelous beauty, her rare intellectual gifts, her fervid eloquence her fearless devotion, and her glorious martyrdom, she stands forth incomparable and immortal amidst her countrywomen."† Ṭáhirih's zeal for her new Faith and her effective teachings in Karbilá alarmed the religious leaders of that city, who complained against her to the civil authorities. The government sent her to Baghdád where she awaited the Sultán's decision regarding her fate. The last three months of her stay in that city was spent in the house of its Mufti, Ibn-i-Alusi. She was eventually informed that she had to return to Iran. 'Abdu'l-Bahá has written:

On a certain day the muftí related one of his dreams, and asked her to tell him what it meant. He said: "In my dream I saw the Shí'ih ulamas arriving at the holy tomb of Imám Ḥusayn, the Prince of Martyrs. They took away the barrier that encloses the tomb, and they broke open the resplendent grave, so that the immaculate body lay revealed to their gaze. They sought to take up the holy form, but I cast myself down on the corpse and I warded them off." Ṭáhirih answered: "This is the meaning of your dream: you are about to deliver me from the hands of the Shí'ih divines." "I too had interpreted it thus," said Ibn-i-Álúsí.

. . . Then came a night when the father of Ibn-i-Álúsí called at the house of his son. He had a meeting with Ṭáhirih and abruptly,

---

* This title was given to Ṭáhirih by Siyyid Káẓim. It means "solace of the eyes."
† Edward Granville Browne, quoted in Nabíl-i-A'ẓam, *The Dawn-Breakers*, p. 629, note 1.

without asking a single question, began to curse, mock and revile her. Embarrassed at his father's behavior, Ibn-i-Álúsí apologized. Then he said: "The answer has come from Constantinople. The King has commanded that you be set free, but only on condition that you leave his realms. Go then, tomorrow, make your preparations for the journey, and hasten away from this land."[14]

# 15

The first eighteen individuals who believed in the Bab were called the Letters of the Living by Him. He gave each of the eighteen a specific mission, a special task. The first to be dispatched in pursuit of his assignment was Mullá 'Alíy-i-Bastámí.* Nabíl-i-A'zam writes:

> The Báb then summoned to His presence Mullá 'Alíy-i-Bastámí, and addressed to him words of cheer and loving-kindness. He instructed him to proceed directly to Najaf and Karbilá, alluded to the severe trials and afflictions that would befall him, and enjoined him to be steadfast till the end. "Your faith," He told him, "must be immovable as the rock, must weather every storm and survive every calamity. Suffer not the denunciations of the foolish and the calumnies of the clergy to afflict you, or to turn you from your purpose. For you are called to partake of the celestial banquet prepared for you in the immortal Realm. You are the first to leave the House of God, and to suffer for His sake. If you be slain in His path, remember that great will be your reward, and goodly the gift which will be bestowed upon you."

No sooner were these words uttered than Mullá 'Alí arose from his seat and set out to prosecute his mission. At about a farsang's† distance from Shíráz he was overtaken by a youth who, flushed with excitement, impatiently asked to speak to him. His name was 'Abdu'l-Vahháb. "I beseech you," he tearfully entreated Mullá 'Alí, "to allow me to accompany you on your journey. Perplexities oppress my heart; I pray you to guide my steps in the way of Truth. Last night, in my dream, I heard the crier announce in the market-street of Shíráz the appearance of the Imám Alí, the Commander of the Faithful. He called to the multitude:

---

* One of the Letters of the Living in the Bábí Faith and its first martyred follower.
† A unit of distance which is about three to four miles.

'Arise and seek him. Behold, he plucks out of the burning fire charters of liberty and is distributing them to the people. Hasten to him, for whoever receives them from his hands will be secure from penal suffering, and whoever fails to obtain them from him, will be bereft of the blessings of Paradise.' Immediately I heard the voice of the crier, I arose and, abandoning my shop, ran across the market-street of Vakíl to a place where my eyes beheld you standing and distributing those same charters to the people. To everyone who approached to receive them from your hands, you would whisper in his ear a few words which instantly caused him to flee in consternation and exclaim: 'Woe betide me, for I am deprived of the blessings of 'Alí and his kindred! Ah, miserable me, that I am accounted among the outcast and fallen!' I awoke from my dream and, immersed in an ocean of thought, regained my shop. Suddenly I saw you pass, accompanied by a man who wore a turban, and who was conversing with you. I sprang from my seat and, impelled by a power which I could not repress, ran to overtake you. To my utter amazement, I found you standing upon the very site which I had witnessed in my dream, engaged in the recital of traditions and verses. Standing aside, at a distance, I kept watching you, wholly unobserved by you and your friend. I heard the man whom you were addressing, impetuously protest: 'Easier is it for me to be devoured by the flames of hell than to acknowledge the truth of your words, the weight of which mountains are unable to sustain!' To his contemptuous rejection you returned this answer: 'Were all the universe to repudiate His truth, it could never tarnish the unsullied purity of His robe of grandeur.' Departing from him, you directed your steps towards the gate of Kázirán. I continued to follow you until I reached this place."[15]

# 16

In *Khadíjih Bagum* by Balyuzi, the wife of the Bab relates: "No words can ever convey my wonderful feeling of good fortune." But, not long after her marriage, she dreamt one night that a fearsome lion was standing in the courtyard of their house, and she herself had her arms around the neck of the lion. The beast dragged her twice round the whole perimeter of the courtyard, and once round half of it. She woke up, alarmed and trembling with fright, and related her dream to her Husband. His comment was: "You awoke too soon. Your dream portends that our life together will not last more than two-and-a-half years." Khadíjih Bagum was greatly distressed, but her Husband's affection and His words of comfort consoled her and prepared her to accept every adversity in the path of God.

# 17

The wife of the Báb, unlike His mother,* perceived at the earliest dawn of His Revelation the glory and uniqueness of His Mission and felt from the very beginning the intensity of its force . . .

To her the Báb confided the secret of His future sufferings, and unfolded to her eyes the significance of the events that were to transpire in His Day. . . . He entrusted her with a special prayer, revealed and written by Himself, the reading of which, He assured her, would remove her difficulties and lighten the burden of her woes. "In the hour of your perplexity," He directed her, "recite this prayer ere you go to sleep. I Myself will appear to you (in the Persian version, it specifies that He will appear to her in her dream) and will banish your anxiety." Faithful to His advice, every time she turned to Him in prayer, the light of His unfailing guidance illumined her path and resolved her problems.[17]

---

* Through the influence of Bahá'u'lláh, the Bab's mother did eventually perceive the glory of her Son's Revelation when she was residing in Karbilá.

# 18

When the Báb was confined, by the order of the governor of the province of Fars, in the house of His uncle Ḥájí Mírzá Siyyid ʿAlí in Shíráz, some of His followers visited Him very cautiously and in secret. William Sears recaps, from *The Dawn-Breakers*, the story of one of His visitors as follows:

One such visitor was a well-known scholar and clergyman named ʿAbduʾl-Karím:*

'Abduʾl-Karím was from the village of Qazvín. He was a merchant, but so great was his longing to know about God that he had given up his business and devoted his life to studying every branch of learning. Because of his great thirst for knowledge, he had soon eclipsed his fellow students. One day he was elevated to the status of teacher. He had qualified himself to speak as an authority on the sacred scriptures of Islam. He was told that he need no longer attend classes, for he now knew as much as the wisest doctor of Islam. Therefore, he, 'Abduʾl-Karím, could now teach others.

At first 'Abduʾl-Karím was elated. But that night, as he began to think about things, his heart was troubled. If he were considered to be among the wisest of all, who was there on earth who really knew anything at all about Almighty God? He knew he was still a victim of cares and worries, of temptations and doubts. Who was he to lead others? He was overcome with a sense of unworthiness. He struggled with these thoughts until dawn, neither eating nor sleeping. He prayed, "Thou seest me, O my Lord, and thou beholdest my plight . . . I am lost in bewilderment at the thought of the multitude of sects into which Thy holy Faith hath fallen. I am deeply perplexed when I behold the schisms that have torn the religions of the past. Wilt Thou guide me in my

---

* He became a secretary of the Báb and was known also as Mírzá Aḥmad-i-Kátib.

perplexities, and relieve me of my doubts?" 'Abdu'l-Karím anguished over the answer to this question.

He relates, "I wept so bitterly that night that I seemed to have lost consciousness. There suddenly came to me the vision of a great gathering of people, the expression of whose shining faces greatly impressed me. A noble figure, attired in the garb of a Siyyid, occupied a seat on the pulpit facing the congregation. He was expounding the meaning of this sacred verse of the Qur'án: 'Whoso maketh efforts for Us, in Our ways will We guide them.' I was fascinated by this face. I arose, advanced towards him, and was on the point of throwing myself at his feet when that vision suddenly vanished. My heart was flooded with light. My joy was indescribable."

'Abdu'l-Karím had consulted a man known throughout the city for his spiritual insight. This man had immediately recognized the Siyyid in the vision as Siyyid Kázim and had told 'Abdu'l-Karím where to find him. 'Abdu'l-Karím had set out at once for Karbilá. There he had found Siyyid Kázim. He had been standing, addressing a crowd, just as 'Abdu'l-Karím had seen him in his dream. He was speaking those very same words. 'Abdu'l-Karím spent an entire winter in close companionship with Siyyid Kázim, who spoke constantly of the coming Messenger.

"The promised One," he would openly and repeatedly declare, "lives in the midst of this people. The appointed time for His appearance is fast approaching. Prepare the way for Him, and purify yourselves so that you may recognize His beauty." Siyyid Kázim said the new Messenger of God would not be recognized until after his death. He implored his followers to arise and seek him without rest.

On the day when 'Abdu'l-Karím parted from Siyyid Kázim, he told him, "Rest assured, O 'Abdu'l-Karím, you are one of those who, in the day of His Revelation, will arise for the triumph of His Cause. You will, I hope, remember me on that blessed Day."

'Abdu'l-Karím returned to his home in Qazvín to await that wonderful day. A few years passed with no sign of the Promised One's coming, but 'Abdu'l-Karím's heart was assured.

He returned to his business as a merchant, but each night he would come home and withdraw to the quiet of his room. He would beseech God with all of his heart, saying, "Thou hast, by the mouth of an inspired servant of Thine, promised that I shall attain unto the presence of Thy Messenger and hear Thy Word. How long wilt Thou withhold me from my promise?" Each night he would renew this prayer and would continue his supplications until the break of day.

One night in February 1840, 'Abdu'l-Karím was deep in prayer, almost in a trance-like state, when something extraordinary occurred. "There appeared before me a bird, white as snow, which hovered above my head and alighted upon the twig of a tree beside me," he has related. "In accents of indescribable sweetness, that bird voiced these words: 'Are you seeking the Manifestation, O 'Abdu'l-Karím? Lo, the year '60.'* Immediately after, the bird flew away and vanished." The memory of the beauty of that vision lingered long in 'Abdu'l-Karím's mind.

A few years went by, but 'Abdu'l-Karím did not forget the message of the bird, and it was always on his mind. Then word came of a wondrous person living in the city of <u>Sh</u>íráz. He left for <u>Sh</u>íráz immediately.

He continued to treasure within his heart the strange message conveyed to him by the bird. When he subsequently attained the presence of the Báb and heard from His lips those same words, spoken in the same tone and language as he had heard them in his vision, he realized their significance.

'Abdu'l-Karím burst into tears and threw himself at the Báb's feet in a state of profound ecstasy, much to the astonishment of his companions. The Báb lovingly took him in His arms, kissed his forehead, and invited him to be seated by His side. In a tone of tender affection, He succeeded in appeasing the tumult of 'Abdu'l-Karím's heart.[18]

---

* Year 1260 A.H., or 1844 A.D.

# 19

Under the order of the tyrannical Ḥusayn Khán, the governor of Fars, the Báb had to leave Shíráz. So, in the summer of 1846, the Báb left His native town, Shíráz, and proceeded to Isfáhán. He resided in that city for about six months, first in the house of its chief priest and then in the residence of Manúchihr Khán, the benevolent governor of Isfáhán, who kept Him safe from the vicious attacks of the clergy. After the death of Manúchihr Khán, his successor was directed by the king to send the Báb to Tihrán. Accordingly, the Báb accompanied by the mounted escort departed Isfáhán, in the dead of the night, and proceeded toward Tihrán. This destination, however, was changed later when the Báb and His escort reached a village near Tihrán. Under the influence of his capricious prime minister, the king reversed his previous decision and wrote to the Báb, asking Him to proceed to Máh-Kú, a remote village in the northwestern corner of Iran. In His march from Isfáhán toward Tihrán, the Báb passed through the old and historic city of Káshán where Ḥájí Mírzá Jání was residing. Nabíl-i-A'ẓam writes:

> On the eve of the Báb's arrival at Káshán, Ḥájí Mírzá Jání,* sur-named Parpá, a noted resident of that city, dreamed that he was stand-ing at a late hour in the afternoon at the gate of 'Aṭṭár, one of the gates of the city, when his eyes suddenly beheld the Báb on horseback wearing, instead of His customary turban, the kuláh† usually worn by the merchants of Persia. Before Him, as well as behind Him, marched a number of horsemen into whose custody He seemed to have been delivered. As they approached the gate, the Báb saluted him and said:

---

* He was the first Bábí in Kashan who was taught by Mullá Ḥusayn-i-Bushrú'í, the first Letter of the Living.

† A Persian hat.

"Ḥájí Mírzá Jání, We are to be your Guest for three nights. Prepare yourself to receive Us."

When he awoke, the vividness of his dream convinced him of the reality of his vision. This unexpected apparition constituted in his eyes a providential warning which he felt it his duty to heed and observe. He accordingly set out to prepare his house for the reception of the Visitor, and to provide whatever seemed necessary for His comfort. As soon as he had completed the preliminary arrangements for the banquet which he had decided to offer the Báb that night, Ḥájí Mírzá Jání proceeded to the gate of 'Aṭṭár, and there waited for the signs of the Báb's expected arrival. At the appointed hour, as he was scanning the horizon, he discerned in the distance what seemed to him a company of horsemen approaching the gate of the city. As he hastened to meet them, his eyes recognized the Báb surrounded by His escort dressed in the same clothes and wearing the same expression as he had seen the night before in his dream. Ḥájí Mírzá Jání joyously approached Him and bent to kiss His stirrups. The Báb prevented him, saying: "We are to be your Guest for three nights. To-morrow is the day of Naw-Rúz; we shall celebrate it together in your home."[19]

# 20

As noted before,* the Bab assigned a specific mission to each of the eighteen Letters of the Living. To Mullá Ḥusayn, the first to believe in Him, He entrusted a special assignment. He directed him to Tihrán, a "city which enshrines a Mystery of such transcendent holiness as neither Ḥijáz nor Shíráz can hope to rival."† Mullá Ḥusayn was to deliver a letter from the Báb to an exalted person, Bahá'u'lláh, in that city.

After successfully completing his historic mission to Tihrán, Mullá Ḥusayn proceeded to Khurásán, according to the Báb's instructions, to continue his teaching work there. At the time when the Báb was incarcerated in the fortress of Máh-Kú, Mullá Ḥusayn decided to visit Him. So, early in the year 1848 he, accompanied by his attendant, Qambar-'Alí, started his journey towards Máh-Kú on foot. He passed through many towns, including Tihrán, where he had the honor of meeting Bahá'u'lláh. 'Alí Khan, the warden of the fortress of Máh-Kú, had a strange dream just before Mullá Ḥusayn reached the fortress. Under the influence of this dream, 'Alí Khan abandoned his harsh and strict rules and was impelled to exhibit much reverence toward the Bab. Nabíl-i-A'zam writes:

> The night before his (Mullá Ḥusayn's) arrival at Máh-Kú, which was the eve of the fourth Naw-Rúz‡ after the declaration of the Mission of the Báb, . . . 'Alí Khan dreamed a dream. "In my sleep," he thus relates his story, "I was startled by the sudden intelligence that Muḥammad, the Prophet of God, was soon to arrive at Máh-Kú, that He was to proceed directly to the castle in order to visit the Báb and to offer Him His congratulations on the advent of the Naw-Rúz festival. In my dream, I ran

---

* See Dream #15.
† Nabíl-i-A'zam, *The Dawn-Breakers*, p. 96.
‡ 1848 A.D.

out to meet Him, eager to extend to so holy a Visitor the expression of my humble welcome. In a state of indescribable gladness, I hastened on foot in the direction of the river, and as I reached the bridge, which lay at a distance of a maydán* from the town of Máh-Kú, I saw two men advancing towards me. I thought one of them to be the Prophet Himself, while the other who walked behind Him I supposed to be one of His distinguished companions. I hastened to throw myself at His feet, and was bending to kiss the hem of His robe, when I suddenly awoke. A great joy had flooded my soul. I felt as if Paradise itself, with all its delights, had been crowded into my heart. Convinced of the reality of my vision, I performed my ablutions, offered my prayer, arrayed myself in my richest attire, anointed myself with perfume, and proceeded to the spot where, the night before in my dream, I had gazed upon the countenance of the Prophet. I had instructed my attendants to saddle three of my best and swiftest steeds and to conduct them immediately to the bridge. The sun had just risen when, alone and unescorted, I walked out of the town of Máh-Kú in the direction of the river. As I approached the bridge, I discovered, with a throb of wonder, the two men whom I had seen in my dream walking one behind the other, and advancing towards me. Instinctively I fell at the feet of the one whom I believed to be the Prophet, and devoutly kissed them. I begged Him and His companion to mount the horses which I had prepared for their entry into Máh-Kú. 'Nay,' was His reply, 'I have vowed to accomplish the whole of my journey on foot. I will walk to the summit of this mountain and will there visit your Prisoner.'"[20]

* A subdivision of a farsakh; it also means a square or open space.

# 21

Men of distinguished merit, eminent members of the clergy, and even government officials were openly and rapidly embracing the Faith of the Báb. Lord Curzon,* in his book, *Persia and the Persian Question*, published in 1892 writes, "The lowest estimate places the present number of Bábís in Persia at half a million. I am disposed to think, from conversations with persons well qualified to judge, that the total is nearer one million. They are to be found in every walk of life, from the ministers and nobles of the Court to the scavenger or the groom, not the least arena of their activity being the Mussulman priesthood itself." We read in *The Dawn-Breakers*:

> It came to pass at that time that a prominent official of high literary ability, Mírzá Asadu'lláh, who was later surnamed Dayyán by the Báb and whose vehement denunciations of His Message had baffled those who had endeavored to convert him, dreamed a dream. When he awoke, he determined not to recount it to anyone, and, fixing his choice on two verses of the Qur'án, he addressed the following request to the Bab: "I have conceived three definite things in my mind. I request you to reveal to me their nature." Mírzá Muḥammad-'Alí† was asked to submit this written request to the Báb. A few days later, he received a reply penned in the Báb's handwriting, in which He set forth in their entirety the circumstances of that dream and revealed the exact texts of those verses. The accuracy of that reply brought about a sudden conversion. Though unused to walking, Mírzá Asadu'lláh hastened on foot along that steep and stony path which led from Khuy to the castle. His friends tried to induce him to proceed on horseback to Chihríq, but he refused their offer. His meeting with the Báb confirmed him in his belief and excited that fiery ardor which he continued to manifest to the end of his life.[21]

---

* A British statesman. He was the viceroy and governor-general of India, 1898–1905.
† A distinguished Siyyid from the city of Khuy who had become a follower of the Báb.

# 22

Nabíl, the historian, has reported the following:

During the Báb's captivity in the castle of <u>Chihríq</u>, events of a startling character caused grave perturbation to the government. It soon became evident that a number of the most eminent among the siyyids, the ulamas, and the government officials of <u>Kh</u>uy had espoused the Cause of the Prisoner and had completely identified themselves with His Faith. . . . A further cause for apprehension on the part of the government authorities was supplied by the arrival at <u>Chihríq</u> of a dervish who had come from India and who, as soon as he met the Bab, acknowledged the truth of His Mission. All who met that dervish, whom the Báb had named Qahru'lláh, during his sojourn at Iskí-<u>Sh</u>ahr,* felt the warmth of his enthusiasm and were deeply impressed by the tenacity of his conviction. An increasing number of people became enamored of the charm of his personality and willingly acknowledged the compelling power of his Faith. Such was the influence which he exercised over them that a few among the believers were inclined to regard him as an exponent of Divine Revelation, although he altogether disclaimed such pretensions. He was often heard to relate the following: "In the days when I occupied the exalted position of navváb† in India, the Báb appeared to me in a vision. He gazed at me and won my heart completely. I arose, and had started to follow Him, when He looked at me intently and said: 'Divest yourself of your gorgeous attire, depart from your native land, and hasten on foot to meet Me in Á<u>dh</u>irbáyján.

---

\* A town situated at an hour's distance from the castle of <u>Chihríq</u>.

† Navváb or Nabob—a provincial governor of the Mogul empire in India, or a person of great wealth or prominence.

In Chihríq you will attain your heart's desire.' I followed His directions and have now reached my goal."

This fulfilled the words of the Islamic tradition that prophesies, "On the last Day, the Men of the Unseen shall, on the wings of the spirit, traverse the immensity of the earth, shall attain the presence of the promised Qá'im, and shall seek from Him the secret that will resolve their problems and remove their perplexities."[22]

# 23

In 1848, eighty-one Bábís gathered in Badasht, a small hamlet near the Caspian Sea. Their primary purpose, according to Shoghi Effendi, was ". . . to implement the revelation of the Bayán by a sudden, a complete and dramatic break with the past."* This event, known as the Conference of Badasht, signalized, in effect, the end of the Adamic cycle and the beginning of the Bahá'í cycle. Meanwhile, Mullá Ḥusayn and his companions set out from Khurásán and proceeded toward Mázindarán to rescue Quddús who, after the conference of Badsht, had been arrested and kept in the house of the leading divine in Sárí.† Near the shrine of Shaykh Tabarsí, Mullá Ḥusayn and his company were ambushed and attacked. To protect themselves from this unprovoked attack, they entered the shrine, then raised a wall and built a fortress around it. For nearly six months, three hundred and thirteen valiant followers of the Báb took refuge in this hastily erected fort‡ and defended themselves against twelve thousand men from the government's army. Eventually, the weakened but courageous survivors responded positively to a false truce and left the safety of the fort. Thereupon, the troops fell upon them and massacred most of the defenseless and trusting heroes of that historic struggle. Nabíl has written:

> The night preceding their [Mullá Ḥusayn and his companions] arrival, the guardian of the shrine dreamed that the Siyyidu'sh-Shuhadá', the Imám Ḥusayn, had arrived at Shaykh Tabarsí, accompanied by no less than seventy-two warriors and a large number of his companions. He dreamed that they tarried in that spot, engaged in the most heroic of

---

* Shoghi Effendi, *God Passes By*, p. 50.
† The capital city of Mázindarán province in northern Iran.
‡ This became known as the Fort of Shaykh Tabarsí, which is located about fourteen miles southeast of the city of Babol in the province of Mázindarán in northern Iran.

battles, triumphing in every encounter over the forces of the enemy, and that the Prophet of God, Himself, arrived one night and joined that blessed company.* When Mullá Ḥusayn arrived on the following day, the guardian immediately recognized him as the hero he had seen in his vision, threw himself at his feet, and kissed them devoutly. Mullá Ḥusayn invited him to be seated by his side, and heard him relate his story. "All that you have witnessed," he assured the keeper of the shrine, "will come to pass. Those glorious scenes† will again be enacted before your eyes." That servant threw in his lot eventually with the heroic defenders of the fort and fell a martyr within its walls.[23]

---

* Bahá'u'lláh soon visited Fort Shaykh Tabarsí for a brief time, and shortly after His visit, Quddús joined Mullá Ḥusayn and his companions at the fort.

† This alludes to the battle in Karbilá in which Imám Ḥusayn was tragically martyred.

# 24

Among the defenders of the Fort of Shaykh Tabarsí were two brothers from Sang-Sar.* The older, Siyyid Aḥmad, was among those who were killed after they left the fort following the false promise of safety by the commander of the attacking army. The younger one, Mír Abu'l-Qásim, was killed on the same night which Mullá Ḥusayn was slain. Their father was Mír Muḥammad-'Alí, a learned and pious man, who was an admirer of Shaykh Aḥmad-i-Aḥsá'í. The year preceding the declaration of the Báb, this man departed for Karbilá with the intention of introducing his two sons to Siyyid Kázim. Before his arrival, however, the Siyyid had departed this world. Right away, he went to Najaf where he had a prophetic dream. Nabíl-i-A'ẓam writes, "While in that city, the Prophet Muḥammad one night appeared to him in a dream, bidding the Imám 'Alí, the Commander of the Faithful, announce to him that after his death both his sons, Siyyid Aḥmad and Mír Abu'l-Qásim, would attain the presence of the promised Qá'im and would each suffer martyrdom in His path. As soon as he awoke, he called for his son Siyyid Aḥmad and acquainted him with his will and last wishes. On the seventh day after that dream he died."[24]

---

* A city located in the Simnan province of Iran on the southern slopes of the Alborz Mountains.

# 25

Zaynab Bagum, her husband, her daughter, and her two sons are reported to have been the earliest residents of Ardistan* to accept the message of the Báb. Soon after the declaration of the Báb, they all traveled to Iṣfahán, where they had the honor of attaining the presence of Mullá Ḥusayn and joining the small band of the early believers.

In the year 1847, the Báb issued an injunction urging all the Bábís to gather under the black standard,† which was being unfurled by Mullá Ḥusayn in Khurásán. Zaynab Bagum's two sons, Mírzá Haydar-'Alí and Mírzá Muḥammad, along with a few other Bábís from Ardistan, heeded this call and proceeded toward Khurásán. All took part in the struggle at Fort of Tabarsí, and all died except Mírzá Haydar-'Alí. He was also wounded by a few gunshots at the village of Dizva, where the government commander and his men treacherously murdered the Bábís who had left the fort after they were promised safety and freedom. After the massacre, the soldiers walked among the fallen victims and, using their swords, killed those who were still breathing. Mírzá Haydar-'Alí was one of those wounded and fallen. A soldier spotted him and went over to finish him off, but when he saw his wonderful face and his green scarf, he had a change of heart. Then he heard the victim reciting quietly a verse from the Qur'án. The soldier's eyes welled up with tears, and he left that abominable scene. The lifeless bodies of the brave and innocent martyrs remained in the square of Dizva village. When the darkness of the night fell and the military camp was removed from the village, Mírzá Haydar-'Alí rose up from among the dead and, with much difficulty, dragged himself to the next village. A Bedouin woman felt pity for him, took him to her tent, and attended to his wounds. He rested and recuperated in the tent

---

* A town situated about 260 miles south of Tihrán and 70 miles northeast of Iṣfahán.
† A Shí'ah Muslim tradition held that the army of the Qá'im would come from Khurásán, under a black banner, to conquer the world.

of that heaven-sent angel for a few days. Then he started his long and arduous homeward march. He had no provisions but plenty of pain from the effect of the bullets. He was afraid to enter any village, approach any person, or go to a suitable place to clean himself. So, on his way back to Ardistan, he suffered greatly. Often he wondered why and for what purpose he was still alive.

One night when he was sleeping in the wilderness, he had a dream in which he saw the Báb. The Báb told Mírzá Haydar-'Alí that he was kept alive so that he could relate the events of Fort Tabarsí for posterity. From that night on, Mírzá Haydar-'Alí was certain that he had an assignment and an obligation to fulfill. He therefore wrote down in detail all the events surrounding the struggle at the Fort of Shaykh Tabarsí for future generations. His written accounts of that defensive undertaking by a relatively small band of intrepid Bábís became one of the references used by Nabíl-i-A'zam, the immortal chronicler of *The Dawn-Breakers*. After a long and agonizing walk, Mírzá Haydar-'Alí eventually reached his hometown. His mother, Zaynab Bagum, would not allow her son into the house. She told him that if he had run away from the fort, he didn't deserve to live in that house. Neither did she want him to be counted as one of her sons any longer. Mírzá Haydar-'Alí had to tell her about the death of his brother and his own dream. He told her that Almighty God had kept him alive so that he could inform the others about the events at Fort Tabarsí. After hearing his story and becoming certain that he was telling the truth, she opened the door and welcomed her son with open arms. After some two years of separation, they held each other and cried copiously for a long time. The believers and the neighbors poured into that house and observed that remarkable reunion. Mírzá Haydar-'Alí lived for many more years and had the bounty of seeing Bahá'u'lláh once in Baghdád and another time in 'Akká. He died during the ministry of 'Abdu'l-Bahá in the year 1905, when he was more than one hundred years old.[25]

# 26

The following is related by Munírih Khánum, the wife of 'Abdu'l-Bahá:

My grandmother (my father's mother) was a holy and pure soul—
may the Lord be with her always! One night in her dream, she saw two
balls of light rising up from the well in her home, and they entered
her heart. This dream excited her so much that she awoke, and stayed
awake all night. Before sunrise, full of happiness, she went to the house
of a preeminent scholar whose word was obeyed throughout Persia; no
one was his equal. My grandmother told him her dream, and asked him
what it meant. He said, "Be happy, for God will give you two children
who will be like suns, and will spread their light on all your family and
relatives."

About then, my grandmother became pregnant; my father was born
first; and a year and three months later, my uncle Hádí was born.[26]

# 27

Two other Bábís who obeyed the injunction of the Báb and left their hometown, Iṣfahán, and proceeded to Khurásán to gather under the black standard were the father of Munírih Khánum and her uncle (the two brothers mentioned in the previous story). Below is her account of their ordeal:

The Báb was taken from Iṣfahán to Tabriz and Máh-Kú. An order was received from Him instructing all the believers to gather under the black standard which was being raised in Khurásán. My father prepared for the journey, and before he left he told my mother (who was expecting me): "I am setting out on a journey. I do not know what the outcome of it will be. Perhaps I will be martyred. So my instruction to you is that if God gives us a child, you should call it 'Alí if it is a boy; and if a girl, then call her Fátimih." This was my father's will as spoken to my mother. He then set out for Khurásán with a group of about twenty-five men. At that time, the Blessed Beauty [Bahá'u'lláh] was at Badasht with Quddús and Ṭáhirih. Every day the believers would gather there from the surrounding areas, until the Badasht conference was over. Then the Army of God set out for Khurásán. It was then that the incidents of Níyálá and the stoning of the believers took place. These events at Níyálá have been recorded at length in books covering the history of the period.* My uncle received severe injuries and died on the way. My father gave the following account of the episode:

When the believers dispersed from Níyálá in groups, each taking a different route, the inhabitants of Níyálá followed them and martyred whoever they could lay their hands on. My brother and I and several other

---

* See, for instance, Nabíl-i-A'ẓam, *The Dawn-Breakers*, pp. 298–300.

people continued on our way [after the attack], when suddenly my brother was overcome with a feeling of great weakness. We arrived at a ruined caravanserai, and here we spent the night. My brother died there, and the other friends, fearing attack by our enemies, each crept away in some direction during the night. So, only I and my brother's corpse remained. In the morning, I left the caravanserai and stood bewildered and confused at the roadside, wondering how to go about burying my brother and how to save my own skin from the enemies. Suddenly, I saw a woman coming toward me from a distance. When she reached me she asked: "Who are you and why are you standing here?" I told her: "My brother died in this caravanserai last night, and I am at a loss as to how to go about burying him." The woman said, "Do not worry about this, for I have come to perform this very service. Last night I dreamt that her holiness Fátimih Zahra,* upon her be peace, said to me, 'One of my children has died in this caravanserai. You must go tomorrow and bury him.' Now, I have come to fulfill her command." She said this and hurried back to her village. She returned a few minutes later with the gravediggers and all that was necessary for a funeral. My brother's body was washed in a stream of water, a shroud was wrapped around him, and, as he had requested that he be buried by the highway which pilgrims take on their way to Karbilá, he was buried right there. The villagers then returned to their homes and I turned toward

---

* The revered daughter of the Prophet Muḥammad and wife of the Imám ʻAlí. The Muslims regard her as the holiest woman in Islám.

Tihrán. From there I continued to Isfáhán in a state of utter exhaustion, having been stoned and badly injured, with my brother dead and the whereabouts of my sister, who was with Ṭáhirih, unknown. In such a condition I entered Isfáhán at a time when it was impossible for anyone even to mention the word Bábí.[27]

# 28

In her book *The Chosen Highway*, Lady Blomfield has written the following story told by 'Abdu'l-Bahá:

There was a woman who was one of the disciples of His Holiness the Báb; she had seven sons; six of them had been martyred. She dreamed a dream, and behold, she saw her seventh son, the only one left. He was being brought to her with a dagger in his heart. When she awoke from her dream she prayed: "O God, the Compassionate! I gave six sons unto Thee. I cannot lose my only son, the last one left to me. Oh spare him! Do not take him also!"

As she prayed, a young woman, who was a friend, came to her:

"Why lamentest thou?" she asked. "I have lost six sons, who were martyred for their Faith. I am begging God not to take my last one," she answered. "If I were worthy, and had beautiful sons, I would give them all to my God," the young friend said.

In course of time a boy, Ashraf, was born to her also. He grew up to be a joy and comfort to his mother. He was loved and admired by all for his beauty, both of body and of soul. When he was about twenty-two years old, he was arrested, having become a disciple of the Báb. He was condemned to be crucified. As he, Ashraf, was being nailed to the cross the people begged him to deny his Master. He steadfastly refused, saying: "Nay, rather do I wish to be sacrificed for my God."

Then his mother was brought to him. She had been told that he denied his faith—this was to her an unspeakable tragedy. But when she saw her beautiful, beloved only child being nailed to the cross, she cried: "My Ashraf! I owe thee to our God. I promised you to Him before you were born. I brought you up and educated you and taught you [holy things] for this day. If you had consented to deny your God, my very motherhood would have cursed you. But now my mother-blessing will follow you into the Presence of our God."

So spake Umm-Ashraf.

Ashraf, who was a tower of strength and an embodiment of stead-fastness, met his death with calm and much serenity.[28]

# 29

Bahá'u'lláh, the Glory of God, was the Founder of the Bahá'í Faith. Bahá'ís believe that He is the Promised One of all ages. He was born in November 1817 in Iran and died, in May 1892, as an exile, in 'Akká, which is located in today's state of Israel. The primary purpose of the Bahá'í Faith is the establishment of the unity of mankind. This unity will be realized through the spiritual forces released by Bahá'u'lláh's Revelation and through the application of His teachings and the social principles He has enunciated. In *The Dawn-Breakers*, Nabíl has written:

> When Bahá'u'lláh was still a child, the Vazír, His father, dreamed a dream. Bahá'u'lláh appeared to him swimming in a vast, limitless ocean. His body shone upon the waters with a radiance that illumined the sea. Around His head, which could distinctly be seen above the waters, there radiated, in all directions, His long, jet-black locks, floating in great profusion above the waves. As he dreamed, a multitude of fishes gathered round Him, each holding fast to the extremity of one hair. Fascinated by the effulgence of His face, they followed Him in whatever direction He swam. Great as was their number, and however firmly they clung to His locks, not one single hair seemed to have been detached from His head, nor did the least injury affect His person. Free and unrestrained, He moved above the waters and they all followed Him.
>
> The Vazír, greatly impressed by this dream, summoned a soothsayer, who had achieved fame in that region, and asked him to interpret it for him. This man, as if inspired by a premonition of the future glory of Bahá'u'lláh, declared: "The limitless ocean that you have seen in your dream, O Vazír, is none other than the world of being. Single-handed and alone, your son will achieve supreme ascendancy over it. Wherever He may please, He will proceed unhindered. No one will resist His march, no one will hinder His progress. The multitude of fishes signi-

fies the turmoil which He will arouse amidst the peoples and kindreds of the earth. Around Him will they gather, and to Him will they cling. Assured of the unfailing protection of the Almighty, this tumult will never harm His person, nor will His loneliness upon the sea of life endanger His safety."

That soothsayer was subsequently taken to see Bahá'u'lláh. He looked intently upon His face, and examined carefully His features. He was charmed by His appearance, and extolled every trait of His countenance. Every expression in that face revealed to his eyes a sign of His concealed glory. So great was his admiration, and so profuse his praise of Bahá'u'lláh, that the Vazír, from that day, became even more passionately devoted to his son. The words spoken by that sooth-sayer served to fortify his hopes and confidence in Him. Like Jacob, he desired only to ensure the welfare of his beloved Joseph, and to surround Him with his loving protection.[29]

# 30

Another dream, which is quite similar to the preceding one, has also been reported in various books.* This one is reported to have been dreamed by Bahá'u'lláh Himself when He was five or six years of age. The similarity of the two dreams arouses suspicions that the two might have been one and the same dream but recalled erroneously by a reporter or two.

When Bahá'u'lláh was a child of five or six years, He dreamt that He was in a garden where huge birds were flying overhead and attacking Him, but they could not harm Him; then went to bathe in the sea, and there he was attacked by fishes, but they too could cause Him no injury. Bahá'u'lláh related this strange dream to His father, Mírzá Buzurg, who sent for a man who claimed to interpret dreams. After making his calculations, he told Mírzá Buzurg that the expanse of the sea was this world in its entirety, and the birds and fishes were the peoples of the world assailing his Son, because He would promulgate something of vital importance related to the minds of men. But they would be powerless to harm Him, for He would triumph over them all to achieve a momentous matter.[30]

---

* Balyuzi, *Bahá'u'lláh: The King of Glory,* p. 19 and Muḥammad-'Alí Faizi, *Hadrat-i Bahá'u'lláh,* p. 18.

# 31

In Yalrud* there lived a mujtahid,† S͟haykh Muḥammad-Taqí, well-famed throughout the land. He had a thousand scholars of divinity around him, whom he taught and, from time to time, presented with a complex question to resolve. Whenever He returned to His home in Tákur, Bahá'u'lláh would usually stop for a while in Yalrud, and here He would visit the mujtahid, who was distantly related to His family. 'Abdu'l-Bahá has described how His own grandmother, who lived in Yalrud, went one day at dawn to the house of the mujtahid to pray. After the morning prayer S͟haykh Muḥammad-Taqí told her that he had some excellent news for her. He had had a dream in which he had found himself outside a house which no one was allowed to enter, because, said the door-keeper, within it the Qá'im of the House of Muḥammad was closeted with Mírzá Ḥusayn-'Alí‡ of Núr. At first the mujtahid had expressed his surprise that the son of a vizier should be so privileged; but on remembering their distant kinship, he had ascribed the privilege to this fact.[31]

---

* Yalrud is a town in Mazandaran province about forty miles north of Tihrán. It was the hometown of Asiyih K͟hánum, the future wife of Bahá'u'lláh.

† Doctor of Law in Islám.

‡ Bahá'u'lláh's given name.

# 32

At another time, <u>Sh</u>ay<u>kh</u> Muḥammad-Taqí had a dream of coming upon a room filled with trunks, which, he was told, belonged to Bahá'u'lláh. On opening one of them, he found it packed with books, and all the lines of those books studded with gems, the brilliance of which awakened him, he said.[32]

# 33

The Báb's duration of ministry, like that of Christ, was quite short. In July 1850, at the age of 31, He was publicly executed in Tabriz, a city in the northwestern part of Iran. In the summer of 1852, a few irresponsible and revengeful followers of the Báb, who were deeply affected and traumatized by the tragedy of His martyrdom, made an unsuccessful attempt on the life of Násiri'd-Din Sháh, the king of Iran. This appalling act of a few ignorant youths gave rise to a frenzied and indiscriminate slaughter of the Bábís. Bahá'u'lláh, who had absolutely no involvement in that evil act, was accused of being its champion, was apprehended and conducted brutally to the Síyáh-Chál, the Black Pit in Tihrán. He was incarcerated in that dark, damp, and foul-smelling subterranean dungeon for four months. During this imprisonment in the Síyáh-Chál, Bahá'u'lláh had a dream of paramount importance. Shoghi Effendi has linked this dream with "the first stirrings of God's Revelation within His (Bahá'u'lláh's) soul."* He writes, 'There, as He (Bahá'u'lláh) Himself has recorded, under the impact of this dream, He experienced the onrushing force of His newly revealed Mission, that "flowed" even as "a mighty torrent" from His "head" to His "breast," whereupon "every limb" of His body "would be set afire."† Below is Bahá'u'lláh's dream in His Own words: "One night, in a dream, these exalted words were heard on every side: 'Verily, We shall render Thee victorious by Thyself and by Thy Pen. Grieve Thou not for that which hath befallen Thee, neither be Thou afraid, for Thou art in safety. Erelong will God raise up the treasures of the earth—men who will aid Thee through Thyself and through Thy Name, wherewith God hath revived the hearts of such as have recognized Him.'"[33]

---

* Shoghi Effendi, *God Passes By*, p. 156.
† Shoghi Effendi, *Citadel of Faith*, p. 101.

# 34

One of Bahá'u'lláh's companions in the Síyáh-Chál was Mírzá 'Abdu'l-Vahháb-i-Shírází. The first dream of this youth, which brought about his acceptance of the Báb's message, was reported earlier in this book (Dream #15). While he was imprisoned in the Síyáh-Chál, he had another spiritual dream that has been related by Bahá'u'lláh in these words:

We were awakened one night, ere break of day, by Mírzá 'Abdu'l-Vahháb-i-Shírází, who was bound with Us to the same chains. He had left Kázimayn and followed Us to Tihrán, where he was arrested and thrown into prison. He asked Us whether We were awake, and proceeded to relate to Us his dream. "I have this night," he said, "been soaring into a space of infinite vastness and beauty. I seemed to be uplifted on wings that carried me wherever I desired to go. A feeling of rapturous delight filled my soul. I flew in the midst of that immensity with a swiftness and ease that I cannot describe." "To-day," We replied, "it will be your turn to sacrifice yourself for this Cause. May you remain firm and steadfast to the end. You will then find yourself soaring in that same limitless space of which you dreamed, traversing with the same ease and swiftness the realm of immortal sovereignty, and gazing with that same rapture upon the Infinite Horizon."

That morning saw the gaoler again enter Our cell and call out the name of 'Abdu'l-Vahháb. Throwing off his chains, he sprang to his feet, embraced each of his fellow-prisoners, and, taking Us into his arms, pressed Us lovingly to his heart. That moment We discovered that he had no shoes to wear. We gave him Our own, and, speaking a last word of encouragement and cheer, sent him forth to the scene of his martyrdom. Later on, his executioner came to Us, praising in glowing language the spirit which that youth had shown. How thankful We were to God for this testimony which the executioner himself had given![34]

# 35

Following His release from the Síyáh Chál, Bahá'u'lláh was banished from Iran to Baghdád, the city of the 'Abbasids, where He arrived in April 1853. At that time there lived in Káshán a youth by the name of Mírzá Áqá Ján. He was the first person who recognized the station of Bahá'u'lláh,* Who, subsequently, chose him to be His amanuensis. In *Bahá'u'lláh, The King of Glory*, Balyuzi has written, "This youth had a dream, in which the Báb appeared, and then he came upon some of the writings of Bahá'u'lláh. Ascertaining that Jináb-i-Bahá was in Baghdád, he made his way to Iraq, and in Karbilá attained His presence . . . he was the first to recognize in the person of Bahá'u'lláh the Promised One of the Bayán—the Promise of All Ages. In later years, Bahá'u'lláh honoured him with the title of Khadimu'lláh—Servant of God."[35]

---

* Shoghi Effendi, *God Passes By*, p. 179.

# 36

Shortly after Bahá'u'lláh's arrival in Baghdád, Mírzá Yahyá, His half-brother, who was very arrogant and extremely jealous of Bahá'u'lláh, arrived in that city too. Noticing the rising prestige of his majestic elder brother among the friends and inhabitants of that city, Mírzá Yahyá became quite resentful and much agitated. He tried to get the Bábís to acknowledge him as their leader, but they paid scant attention to him. He was alarmed by the reverence and recognition accorded to his half-brother and, in his desperation, asserted that Bahá'u'lláh was preventing the acknowledgment of his position by the people. The lies, accusations and demeaning actions of him and his cohorts caused many difficulties and much confusion in Baghdád. To prevent any further deterioration of the situation and to safeguard the unity among the members of the small band of the Bábí community in Iraq, Bahá'u'lláh decided to leave Baghdád. One morning, the household of Bahá'u'lláh awoke to find Him gone. And no one knew where to seek Him. He had departed to the wilderness of Sulaymaniyyih in the heart of Kurdish 'Iraq. There He lived a life of seclusion for two years, much of which was spent on a mountain named Sargalu.

When Bahá'u'lláh lived on Sargalu Mountain, one of the Shaykhs from Sulaymaniyyeh had a garden in that area (Sargalu). From time to time, he would go there for a visit and inspection. One day when he was resting there, he saw, in his dream, the prophet Muhammad, Who told him to go to the Sargalu Mountain and observe the Light of the Countenance of God. As soon as he woke up, he proceeded to Sargalu Mountain. There he began searching and looking around. Suddenly, he heard the sound of someone chanting a prayer. He advanced toward the sound, which led him to Bahá'u'lláh. The Shaykh hurried toward Him and narrated his dream to Him. Bahá'u'lláh responded by telling him not to be too surprised. As the result of this visit, the Shaykh became attracted to Bahá'u'lláh and asked His permission to visit Him from time to time and to bring some bread for His blessed Person. Bahá'u'lláh accepted his request. This incident passed from tongue to tongue, and it soon became known in Sulaymaniyyeh that an Iranian Dervish,* known as Dervish Muḥammad, was living on Sargalu Mountain under very austere conditions.[36]

---

* A Muslim, often a mystic, who renounces the world and communes with God, subsisting on the charity of his fellow-men.

# 37

Sha<u>ykh</u> 'Abdu'l-Ḥusayn-i-Tihrání, entitled Sha<u>ykh</u>u'l-'Iraqayn, was an implacable enemy of Bahá'u'lláh. He was sent to Karbilá by Náṣiri'd-Dín <u>Sh</u>áh to supervise the repairs of the holy shrines. At the time of Bahá'u'lláh's residency in Ba<u>gh</u>dád, this man, with the collaboration of Mírzá Buzurg <u>Kh</u>án, the Persian Consul-General in Ba<u>gh</u>dád, did his best to uproot the Cause of God and destroy its Author. Bahá'u'lláh's banishment from Ba<u>gh</u>dád became a reality mainly due to the lies and the machinations of these two crafty individuals who were assisted by a number of other religious leaders. One day, Sha<u>ykh</u> 'Abdu'l-Ḥusayn related his dream to his cohorts.

"In my dream," he said, "I saw the king of Iran sitting under a dome. He said to me, 'O Sha<u>ykh</u>, be certain of this, that my sword will eliminate the Bahá'ís altogether.' On the dome, under which the king was sitting, was written the Ayatu'l-Kursi* in English."

The Blessed Beauty sent him the following message through Zaynu'l-Abidin Khan, Fakhru'd-dawlih,† "Your dream is a prophetic one, because Ayatu'l-Kursi is the very same verse as in the Qur'án, although written in English. It means that this Faith is the same as Islam but the script has changed. That is, the words are different but the reality and the true meaning remain the same. As regards that dome, it signifies the cause of God, which is surrounding and overseeing the king. The king is in the shelter of the divine Cause, which is truly victorious."[37]‡

---

* Qur'án 2:255. This verse is usually recited by Muslims for protection.

† A Persian prince who was an admirer of Bahá'u'lláh and who often visited Him.

‡ Years later, at a gathering in Egypt, 'Abdu'l-Bahá, referring to that dream, made a comment to the effect that the dreaming <u>Sh</u>aykh and the king were both gone and forgotten, while more and more people were enlisting under the banner of Bahá'u'lláh.

# 38

During the last years of His residency in Baghdád, Bahá'u'lláh made some veiled remarks about the approaching period of difficulty and tribulation. These hints, together with His apparent concern and grief, caused much apprehension and sorrow among His companions. It was during this anxiety-ridden period that the Tablet of the Holy Mariner* was revealed by Bahá'u'lláh and chanted by His amanuensis among the friends (March 27, 1863). In this Tablet, Bahá'u'lláh "prophesies the severe afflictions that are to befall Him."† The revelation of this Tablet further deepened the feeling of sorrow and disquietude among the friends. In *The Revelation of Bahá'u'lláh*, Taherzadeh writes, "Indeed, on the day following its revelation, the grievous news of the Sultán's decision to call Bahá'u'lláh to Constantinople reached Him; it was news which dealt a crippling blow to every man, woman and child among His lovers in Iraq."‡ It was during these troubled and uncertain times that Bahá'u'lláh had a dream, which is related in the following words by Shoghi Effendi:

A dream which He had at that time, the ominous character of which could not be mistaken, served to confirm the fears and misgivings that had assailed His companions. "I saw," He wrote in a Tablet, "the Prophets and the Messengers gather and seat themselves around Me, moaning, weeping and loudly lamenting. Amazed, I inquired of them the reason, whereupon their lamentation and weeping waxed greater, and they said unto me: 'We weep for Thee, O Most Great Mystery, O Tabernacle of Immortality!' They wept with such a weeping that I

---

\* The main theme of this Tablet is the Covenant.
† Shoghi Effendi, *God Passes By*, p. 221.
‡ Taherzadeh, *The Revelation of Bahá'u'lláh*, 1:243.

too wept with them. Thereupon the Concourse on high addressed Me saying: '. . . Erelong shalt Thou behold with Thine own eyes what no Prophet hath beheld. . . . Be patient, be patient.' . . . They continued addressing Me the whole night until the approach of dawn."[38]

# 39

In one of His dreams, Bahá'u'lláh found Himself associating with the Prophet Muḥammad, Whose utterance concurred with the principle of progressive revelation. Bahá'u'lláh has written copiously on this subject. Here is a sample: "The All-Knowing Physician hath His finger on the pulse of mankind. He perceiveth the disease, and prescribeth, in His unerring wisdom, the remedy. Every age hath its own problem and every soul its particular aspiration. The remedy the world needeth in its present-day afflictions can never be the same as that which a subsequent age may require. Be anxiously concerned with the needs of the age ye live in, and center your deliberations on its exigencies and requirements."* 'Abdu'l-Bahá states, "Religion is the outer expression of the divine reality. Therefore it must be living, vitalized, moving and progressive. If it be without motion and non-progressive it is without the divine life; it is dead."†

In a Tablet, Bahá'u'lláh describes one of His dreams in which He was associating with the Prophet Muḥammad, Who was making some pronouncements. In the course of His exposition and utterances, He made the remark to the effect that He had previously declared that paradise is under the shade of swords. He then continued that, had He been manifested at the time of Bahá'u'lláh's appearance, He would have said that paradise is under the shade of the tree of friendship and mercy. After hearing these words from the mouth of the Apostle of God, Bahá'u'lláh praised Him profusely.

Bahá'u'lláh further adds that His happiness, after waking up from His dream, was beyond any description.

---

* Bahá'u'lláh, *Gleanings from the Writings of Bahá'u'lláh*, no. 106.1.
† 'Abdu'l-Bahá, *The Promulgation of Universal Peace*, p. 194.

# 40

Siyyid Yaḥyáy-i-Dárábí, surnamed Vaḥíd, was, according to Shoghi Effendi "one of the most erudite, eloquent and influential"* followers of the Báb. After accepting the Báb, Vaḥíd became very active in proclaiming His mission. Throngs of people followed and joined him wherever he went. This was especially the case when he reached his hometown of Nayríz, a small town in the province of Fars in southern Iran. The devotion and the fidelity which were extended by a growing number of people to Vaḥíd did not fail to augment the fury and the jealousy which were smoldering in the chest of Zaynu'l-'Abidín Khán, the governor of the town. Soon he managed to organize a thousand-man strong army and planned to capture Vaḥíd with a sudden onslaught. When informed of the governor's plans, Vaḥíd and his followers occupied a nearby fort, and an armed struggle ensued. At the end, Vaḥíd accepted the offer of truce which was extended to him by the governor. Subsequently, he and many of his followers were treacherously massacred. Ḥájí Muḥammad-Taqí was one of those followers who providentially survived the upheaval of Zanján and later became a staunch follower of Bahá'u'lláh. Concerning this brave and tested believer, Balyuzi has written:

> The story of Ḥájí Muḥammad-Taqí, whom Bahá'u'lláh later honoured with the designation of Ayyub (Job), is both moving and awe-inspiring. He survived the holocaust of Nayríz and fell into the clutches of Zaynu'l-'Abidín Khán, the sadistic and greedy governor of that town, who had helped himself copiously to the riches of the wealthy Ḥájí. Every day, as the Governor sat watching and mocking him, he was thrown into an ice-cold pool, battered on the head every time he surfaced, then dragged out and mercilessly lashed (to the accompaniment of the Governor's evident enjoyment and laughter) until blood poured out of

* Shoghi Effendi, *God Passes By*, p. 17.

his wounds. In response to Zaynu'l-'Abidín Khán's jeers, Ḥájí Muḥammad-Taqí praised God for the bounty of suffering in His path. At last, the Governor tired of his satanic pleasures and decided to get rid of the Ḥájí. But the Governor's men proved more God-fearing.* They let Ḥájí Muḥammad-Taqí go, and told him to take himself away as soon and as far as he could, lest he should be discovered alive by their master.

Ḥájí Muḥammad-Taqí, covered with wounds, was so badly beaten and tortured that he could scarcely move. Somehow he managed to drag himself to the outskirts of Nayríz before dropping to the ground like a lifeless body, where he fell asleep. The following story, taken from *Stories of Bahá'u'lláh* written by Furutan, is the one that has been related by Ḥájí Muḥammad-Taqí himself:

> "While sleeping, I dreamed about the Ancient Beauty (Bahá'u'lláh). Even though I had never seen Him, yet I was certain that this was He, and that He was in Baghdad. He addressed these words to me: 'Despite the injuries heaped upon you, We extended Our protection that you might remain alive. Be not grieved, and come to Me in Baghdad.' 'But I have no money,' I replied, 'nor am I able to stand on my feet.' 'You do rely upon God?' were His next words, to which I replied, 'I have always relied upon God.'
>
> "At this point I awoke, and to my great amazement saw that a caravan had set up camp on the banks of the very river beside which I had been sleeping. It turned out that they were pilgrims traveling to Karbilá, many of

---

* It is reported that it was actually the governor's wife who, influenced by a gloomy dream, was impelled to arrange for the release of her husband's prisoner. She secured the assistance of some of the governor's men who helped her in her benevolent undertaking.

whom had come on foot from Kirman. Someone emerged from a tent and, to my great surprise, came straight over to me, and asked me to follow him. Overcome with astonishment, I remained rooted to the spot. He repeated his words. I followed him and we entered the tent. There I saw that several people were attending a man of striking appearance who, as a sign of respect to me, arose and then seated me next to himself. 'During the night,' he told me, 'I dreamed that the Imam Husayn had entrusted to my care a person with the same appearance and features which I behold in you, and he told me, "This Haji is my guest. He should accompany you to Karbilá." So, you are my guest as far as Karbilá.' And so, without the usual formalities of introduction, this distinguished gentleman took me with him, and he would often remark: 'The Imam has guided you to me, and has emphasized that you be shown the utmost hospitality.'

"When we reached Baghdad I told him, 'This is where we part.' He replied that I was to accompany him as far as Karbilá, but I explained that 'the same blessed Personage Who entrusted me to your care also came to me in a dream and invited me to come to Baghdad. Therefore, I shall remain here, and will not continue the journey to Karbilá.' My host paled as he heard these words, and in a very apologetic manner replied: 'To be truthful, the Imam Husayn had directed me to take you as for as Baghdad.' And, with the utmost kindness, he bade me farewell.

"When I came into the presence of the Blessed Beauty, I recognized Him as that same holy Personage Whom I had seen in my dream, and I was favoured with His limitless grace."

Later, the Súrih of Sabr (Patience) was revealed for this same Hájí Muḥammad-Taqí. He passed away in Adrianople during the last days of Bahá'u'lláh's stay in that city.[40]

# 41

'Áqá Rida, a native of <u>Sh</u>íráz and a confectioner (Qannad) by trade, was a devout follower of Bahá'u'lláh, and was closely beside Him from His Bagh-dád days until His ascension. He later served 'Abdu'l-Bahá with equal zeal and devotion, until his death in 1912, while 'Abdu'l-Bahá was in America. When the news of his death reached 'Abdu'l-Bahá, He remarked that He must build Áqá Rida's grave with His own hands, and stand and pray before it. Balyuzi writes:

Áqá Rida recounts the delicious tale of a dream he had in those early days in Istanbul. He says he dreamt that Bahá'u'lláh had written a book, which was held by someone in a public square. And there was a mill which people wanted to set going, but the mill would only move in jerks—stop, then move, then stop again. Someone told Bahá'u'lláh of Áqá Rida's dream. That day, towards sunset, when Bahá'u'lláh was about to leave the house and visit the mosque, Áqá Rida went into His presence. Bahá'u'lláh told him, smiling, that he should endeavour to set the mill going. And Áqá Rida relates that for some time (even in the days of Adrianople) Bahá'u'lláh would occasionally turn to him and say "the mill did not get started."[41]

# 42

Bahá'u'lláh's stay in Adrianople lasted about four years and nine months. Toward the end of this period, He sent Nabíl-i-A'ẓam, one of His Apostles* and the author of *The Dawn-Breakers*, to Egypt on a mission. The Iranian Consul-General in Cairo, who was an obstinate enemy of the Faith, leveled false accusations against Nabíl and urged the Egyptian authorities to imprison him. Nabíl was arrested and thrown into a prison in Cairo and was, subsequently, transferred to another prison in Alexandria.† There, he befriended another inmate, Fáris Effendi, who was a doctor and a Christian clergyman. As a result of his discussions with Nabíl, Fáris accepted the Faith and became a devoted follower of Bahá'u'lláh. It is believed that he was the first Christian to become a Bahá'í. In prison and cut-off from the outside world, Nabíl was quite unaware of the fate of Bahá'u'lláh and His impending banishment to 'Akká. Balyuzi relates Nabíl's story in these words:

> One night, in the early hours of the morning, I (Nabil) saw the Blessed Perfection (Bahá'u'lláh) in the world of dreams. He said: 'Some people have come, asking for permission to harm Mírzá Hasan Khán;‡ what sayest thou?' When I awoke I knew that something would happen that day. I went to Sayyid-na Husayn Square, and walked about for an hour or two. Then I found myself surrounded by a number of people who said, "They have asked for you at the Seraye (government house)." But instead they took me to the house of Mírzá Hasan Khán. Then I realized that they had duped me by mentioning the Seraye, so that I should give myself up, and not say that I was not a Persian subject. After long talks with the Consul, I was handed over to an official, who put me in chains.[42]

---

* Shoghi Effendi designated nineteen eminent early followers of Bahá'u'lláh, the founder of the Bahá'í Faith, as His Apostles.

† The second largest city in Egypt and its largest seaport.

‡ The Persian Consul General in Cairo, a ruthless enemy of the Faith.

# 43

While Nabíl was in prison in Egypt, one night Bahá'u'lláh appeared to him in a dream and assured him that after eighty-one days the hardships of prison life would come to an end. That day fell on Thursday, 27 August 1868,* and it was on that day that the significance of Nabíl's dream came to light. Around the time of sunset he went on the roof of the prison (in Alexandria) and began to watch people passing by. Not long after he had settled in a corner on the roof, to his amazement Nabíl sighted Áqá Muḥammad Ibráhím-i-Náẕir among the passers-by, escorted by a guard. Áqá Muḥammad Ibráhím used to do the work of catering for Bahá'u'lláh and His companions in Adrianople. Now in Alexandria he had left the ship to purchase provisions for the journey. Not knowing anything about Bahá'u'lláh's exile to 'Akká, the astonished Nabíl called out to Muḥammad Ibráhím who succeeded in persuading his guard to allow him to visit his friend in the prison. There he told him of the fate of Bahá'u'lláh and His companions and pointed to the ship which carried the exiles and could be seen from the prison.

This amazing incident caused great agitation in the heart of Nabíl, for he found himself so close to his Beloved and yet so far. When Fáris Effendi was informed, he too became highly excited but frustrated at not being able to attain the presence of His Lord.

That night neither of the two could sleep. Both decided to write a letter to Bahá'u'lláh and the next morning Fáris Effendi made arrangements with a certain Christian youth, Constantine, who was a watchmaker in the city, to deliver their letters to Bahá'u'lláh on board the ship. They both stood on the roof of the prison to watch the ship, turned their hearts to Bahá'u'lláh and communed with His spirit with much devotion and love.

---

* According to the shipping records, the Austrian Lloyd steamer was due to leave Gallipoli on 21 August 1868 and was due in Alexandria on Wednesday 26 August early in the morning. Bahá'u'lláh and His companions transshipped to another steamer of the same company in Alexandria bound for Cyprus via Haifa, which sailed on Friday 28 August.

After a short while they were heartbroken to see the ship steaming away before Constantine could gain admittance. But amazingly, after a few minutes the ship stopped and Constantine, who was in a rowing boat, reached it and went aboard. He handed the envelope to one of the attendants who took it to Bahá'u'lláh. The news of Nabíl's whereabouts, and especially the letter of Fáris, which was read aloud by Bahá'u'lláh to those who had assembled in His presence, created great excitement on board the ship. Bahá'u'lláh revealed a Tablet in honour of Nabíl in which He bestowed His bounties and blessings upon Fáris, and assured him that soon he would be released from the prison. He then called the messenger to His presence, and handed him the Tablet with loving kindness and affection. 'Abdu'l-Bahá and the Purest Branch* also sent some gifts to Nabíl.

This short visit made an abiding impression upon Constantine. Having come face to face for a brief period with the Supreme Manifestation of God, and seen a glimpse of His glory, he left the ship overwhelmed and awestruck. When he came to deliver the parcel to Fáris Effendi, he was in such a state of excitement that he was heard shouting aloud, "By God, I have seen the face of the Heavenly Father." In a state of ecstasy and rapture Fáris embraced Constantine and kissed his eyes which had gazed upon the countenance of his Lord. The Tablet of Bahá'u'lláh was in the handwriting of His amanuensis Mírzá Áqá Ján in the form of "Revelation Writing."† It imparted a new spirit of love and dedication to Fáris; it fanned into flame the fire of faith which had been ignited in his heart by Nabíl in that gloomy prison. As promised by Bahá'u'lláh, Fáris was released from prison three days later. After his release he arose in the propagation of the Faith among his people. Nabíl was also freed soon after, but being ordered to leave Egypt he proceeded to the Holy Land in pursuit of his Lord.

---

* Mírzá Mihdí, Bahá'u'lláh's youngest son from His marriage to His wife Navváb.
† Writing that was taken down as Bahá'u'lláh was revealing the Word of God. Because of the speed of the writing, it would be illegible to all except Mírzá Áqá Ján, who would then rewrite it in legible script.

# 44

As a youth, Ḥájí Mírzá Haydar-'Alí became a follower of the Báb in Isfahán. Subsequently, he accepted the Baháʼí Faith and became a deep and prominent Baháʼí teacher. He traveled and taught the Faith for many years. At the bidding of Baháʼuʼlláh, he traveled to Egypt, where he was arrested and sent to Sudan where he was kept as a prisoner for nine years. In his old age, he was residing in the Holy Land and was known to the Western pilgrims as the Angel of Mount Carmel. On 'Abdu'l-Bahá's suggestion, Mírzá Haydar-'Alí wrote his memoirs under the title of *Bihjatuʼs-Sudúr*, which means *the delight of hearts*. The Hand of the Cause, Mr. A. Faizi, translated into English some sections of this book, which was published under the title *Stories from the Delights of Hearts*. In *Bihjatuʼs-Sudúr*, Ḥájí Mírzá Haydar-'Alí has related that he, as a new believer, had his full share of doubts and uncertainties. He tried by every means to relieve himself from his wayward thoughts. He often went through the cycle of certainty and perplexity. Then one night he had a dream which made him assured and joyous for the rest of his life. Ḥájí Mírzá Haydar-'Alí has written about his reassuring dream in *Bihjatuʼs-Sudúr*. Its English version is recorded in Taherzadeh's *Revelation of Baháʼuʼlláh*, volume 2:

> Then one night I dreamt that a town-crier in . . . Isfahán was announcing this message: "O people, the Seal of the Prophets (Prophet Muḥammad) is here in a certain house and has given permission for anyone who wishes to attain His presence to go there. Remember that a mere glance at His countenance is more meritorious than service in both worlds." On hearing this, I hastened and entered the house. I had never seen such a building. I went upstairs and arrived in an area which had a roof over it and was surrounded by rooms and chambers. The Manifestation of the All-Glorious was pacing up and down and some people were standing motionless. I arrived and spontaneously prostrated myself at His feet. Graciously, He lifted me up with His own hands and, standing, said "A person may claim that he has come

here wholly for the sake of God, and has truly attained the presence of His Lord, when he is not held back by the onslaught of the peoples of the world, who with drawn swords attack him and intend to take his life because he has embraced the Cause of God. Otherwise, he cannot truthfully say that his motive was to seek God."

On hearing these words, I woke up from my dream and found myself assured, joyous and thankful. All my doubts had completely disappeared. . . .

However, time passed, and about fourteen years later I was in the "Land of Mystery" (Adrianople) where I stayed for seven months. Every day, through His bounty, I used to attain the presence of Bahá'u'lláh once, twice and sometimes more. But during this period, I never thought of my dream. One evening about four or five hours after sunset I was sitting . . . in the tea-room [a room set aside for Bahá'u'lláh's companions and visitors]. That day I had not attained the presence of Bahá'u'lláh and was most eager for an opportunity to do so. Although I could never bring myself to ask for permission, in my innermost heart I was entreating and invoking Him for this honor. But there was no hope, for it was far too late. Suddenly, the door opened and the Most Great Branch, ['Abdu'l-Bahá], Who in those days was known as Sirru'lláh [the Mystery of God], entered and summoned me to follow Him. When I came out of the room, I saw the Ancient Beauty [Bahá'u'lláh] pacing in the roofed area of the house. The stream of His utterance was flowing and a few souls were standing. I prostrated myself at His feet, whereupon He lifted me up with His blessed hands. He turned to me and said: "A person may claim that he has arrived here wholly for the sake of God, and has truly attained the presence of His Lord, when he is not held back by the onslaught of the peoples of the world, who with drawn swords attack him and intend to take his life because he has embraced the Cause." These were exactly the words I had heard fourteen years before, and I saw the same incomparable Beauty and the same building as in my dream. I stood by the wall, awe-struck and motionless. Gradually, I recovered and in a state of full consciousness attained His presence. My purpose in telling this story was not, God forbid, to attribute any miracles, but rather to state the facts as they happened . . .[44]

# 45

Mírzá ʿAlí-Muḥammad, surnamed Varqá (Dove) was an eminent early Baháʾí and a great poet who was born in Yazd, Iran. Throughout his accomplished and saintly life, he sang the praises of Baháʾuʾlláh and ʿAbduʾl-Bahá. He and his twelve-year-old son, Rúhuʾlláh, were ruthlessly murdered in a Tihrán jail. Varqá was posthumously designated as a Hand of the Cause of God* by ʿAbduʾl-Bahá and was later named, by Shoghi Effendi, as one of the Apostles of Baháʾuʾlláh. One of his sons, Valíyuʾlláh Varqá, was for many years a member of the National Spiritual Assembly of the Baháʾís in Iran. In 1938 he was appointed by Shoghi Effendi as the Trustee of Huqúquʾlláh (right of God), and in 1951 he was elevated to the rank of the Hand of Cause of God. After his death in 1955, Shoghi Effendi appointed his son, Dr. ʿAlí-Muḥammad Varqá, to the same two positions that had become vacant by the death of his father. Dr. ʿAlí-Muḥammad Varqá (1911–2007) was the last surviving Hand of the Cause of God. In *The Revelation of Baháʾuʾlláh*, Taherzadeh writes:

On his first pilgrimage in AH 1296 (AD 1878–79) . . . Varqá came in contact with the divine spirit and was utterly magnetized by the onrushing forces of Baháʾuʾlláh's Revelation. He truly became a new creation and emerged as one of the spiritual giants of this age. The first time he gazed upon the face of His Lord he was surprised, because he thought that he had previously seen Him somewhere, but he could not remember the occasion or the place. He was puzzled by this until one day after several times coming into His presence, Baháʾuʾlláh said to him, "Varqá! Burn away the idols of vain imaginings!" On hearing

---

* Hands of the Cause of God were a distinguished group of Baháʾís who were chosen by the Central Figures of the Baháʾí Faith. Their main functions were to propagate and to protect the Faith.

these words, Varqá immediately recalled a dream he had had when he was a child. He was in a garden playing with some dolls when "God" arrived, took the dolls from him and burned them in the fire. When he told this dream to his parents they pointed out to him that no one can see God. However, he had completely forgotten this dream until that day when the words of Bahá'u'lláh exhorting him to burn the idols aroused his memory, and he knew that he had seen Bahá'u'lláh in his dream as a child.[45]

# 46

In *God Passes By*, Shoghi Effendi writes, "Even the Mufti of 'Akká, <u>Sh</u>ay<u>kh</u> Maḥmúd, a man notorious for his bigotry, had been converted to the Faith, and, fired by his newborn enthusiasm, made a compilation of the Muḥammadan traditions related to 'Akká."* Here is the story of this man's conversion as written by Adib Taherzadeh:

<u>Sh</u>ay<u>kh</u> Maḥmúd was one of the religious leaders of 'Akká when Bahá'u'lláh was exiled to that city. He was born into a family of devout Muslims. When he was about ten years of age, an old <u>Sh</u>ay<u>kh</u>, a religious man revered by Maḥmúd's father, had a vision of the coming of the Person of the "Promised One" to 'Akká. He intimated this to Maḥmúd in the presence of his father and told him that his father and himself were old men and would not live to see that day. But he assured Maḥmúd that he would then be a grown-up person and bade him watch out for the coming of the Lord. He even indicated to Maḥmúd that He would speak in the Persian tongue and reside in an upper room at the top of a long flight of stairs.

Some years passed and the young boy grew up into a strong man, learned and pious, well respected by the community and known as <u>Sh</u>ay<u>kh</u> Maḥmúd. But he seldom thought of the vision, and when Bahá'u'lláh came to 'Akká it never occurred to him that He might be the One foretold by the old <u>Sh</u>ay<u>kh</u>. On the contrary, he deeply resented the action of the Government in sending Bahá'u'lláh, whom the authorities had described as an evil man and the "God of the Persians," to the city of 'Akká. For some time he was in a state of agitation, wanting to do something to rid the city of such a person. . . . One day he hid a weapon under his cloak and went straight to the barracks with the intention of assassinating Bahá'u'lláh. He informed the guards

---

* Shoghi Effendi, *God Passes By*, pp. 303–4.

at the prison gate that he wished to see Bahá'u'lláh. Since he was an influential personality in 'Akká, the guards complied with his request and went to inform Bahá'u'lláh of the identity of the visitor. "Tell him," Bahá'u'lláh is reported to have said, "to cast away the weapon and then he may come in."* On hearing this Shaykh Maḥmúd was astounded, for he was sure that no one had seen the weapon under his cloak. In a state of utter confusion he returned home, but his agitated mind could not be at rest. He continued in this state for some time until he decided to go to the barracks again, but without any weapons this time. Being a strong man he knew he could take Bahá'u'lláh's life by the mere strength of his hands.

So he went again to the prison gate and made the same request to visit Bahá'u'lláh. On being informed of Shaykh Maḥmúd's desire to meet Him, Bahá'u'lláh is reported to have said: "Tell him to purify his heart first and then he may come in."† Perplexed and confused at these utterances, Shaykh Maḥmúd could not bring himself to visit Bahá'u'lláh that day. Later he had a dream in which his father and the old Shaykh appeared to him and reminded him of their vision regarding the coming of the Lord. After this dream Shaykh Maḥmúd went to the barracks again and attained the presence of 'Abdu'l-Bahá. The words of the Master penetrated his heart and he was ushered into the presence of Bahá'u'lláh. The majesty and glory of His countenance overwhelmed the Shaykh and he witnessed the fulfilment of the prophecy of the coming of the Lord to 'Akká. He prostrated himself at His feet and became an ardent believer.[46]

---

* These are not the exact words of Bahá'u'lláh but convey the message he is reported to have given.

† These are not the exact words of Bahá'u'lláh but convey the message he is reported to have given.

# 47

In 1839 many Jews living in the city of Mashhad were massacred and the surviving ones accepted Islám in order to save their lives. Despite their conversion, they were secretly practicing their Jewish Faith and were not fully accepted by the Muslims or integrated into the society. Mírzá 'Azízu'lláh and his family lived in such a community. One day he heard the name of Bahá'u'lláh and the story of Badí'* from his brother who had become a Bahá'í. But Mírzá 'Azízu'lláh was not interested and remained steadfast in his Jewish Faith. Even after reading a Bahá'í book and being moved by its contents, he could not come to terms with the idea of a new religion. Then one night he had a spiritual dream the account of which he has written in his memoirs. The English translation of this account appears in *The Revelation of Bahá'u'lláh* by Taherzadeh:

> In my dream, I heard the announcement that the Lord of Hosts, the Promised One of all ages, had appeared, and that He was inspecting the company of the Prophets and all their followers. I went along immediately to the appointed place. I saw a vast place on which multitudes of people were assembled in lines. Each prophet along with his followers was seated facing the Qiblih.† I was surprised by the extraordinary light and vision which was given to my eyes, as I could easily see all the people lined up in that vast area.
>
> Opposite the multitudes and facing them, a venerable figure was seated upon a chair uttering some words. I was standing at the end of a line. His blessed Person was over fifty years of age, had a long black beard and was wearing a green Táj‡ sewn with green silk thread.

---

* The heroic youth who was the bearer of Bahá'u'lláh's Tablet to Naṣiri'd-Dín Sháh and who was subsequently martyred. Bahá'u'lláh gave him the title *The Pride of Martyrs*.
† Literally: point of adoration. A point to which the faithful turn at the time of prayer.
‡ Literally meaning *crown*; a head-dress similar to the ones Bahá'u'lláh used.

With His blessed hand He signaled me to go to Him. With my hands I gesticulated to say, how can I come with all these crowds in front of me? He waved His hands to the multitudes and they all prostrated themselves on the ground. He then beckoned me to go forward. I was not sure at this point whether it was to me or someone else that He was signaling. He then repeated His command. This time I went forward immediately, stepping on the backs of people who lay prostrate in front of me, until I reached Him. I prostrated myself at His feet and kissed them. He then helped me up to my feet with His hand and recited the verse of the Qur'án: "Blessed be God, the most excellent Creator."*

Although this dream made a great impression on Mírzá 'Azízu'lláh, he still remained steadfast in his Jewish faith until some time later when he was converted to the Faith of Bahá'u'lláh by Ḥájí 'Abdu'l-Majíd, the father of Badí'.† Soon after embracing the Faith, Mírzá 'Azízu'lláh and his brother journeyed to 'Akká to attain the presence of Bahá'u'lláh. This was in the year 1876, his first pilgrimage to the Holy Land. When the appointed time arrived, Mírzá 'Azízu'lláh was ushered into the room of Bahá'u'lláh in 'Akká. As soon as his eyes saw the person of Bahá'u'lláh he was awestruck to find himself in the presence of the One whom he had seen some years before in that memorable dream, wearing the same clothes and the same green head-dress. With all the devotion and love in his heart Mírzá 'Azízu'lláh promptly prostrated himself at the feet of his Lord. Bahá'u'lláh bent down, helped him up to his feet and recited the verse of the Qur'án: "Blessed be God, the most excellent Creator!"[47]

---

* Qur'án, 23:14.
† See the following story.

# 48

Ḥájí ʻAbduʼl-Majíd-i-Níshápúrí was one of the survivors of the bloody struggles at Fort Shaykh Ṭabarsí and the father of The Pride of Martyrs, Áqá Buzurg, entitled Badíʻ. As a Bábí, when he first heard of Baháʼuʼlláhʼs Declaration, he happily and without any hesitation joined the ranks of the Baháʼís and began serving the Cause. At an advanced age of eighty-four, Ḥájí ʻAbduʼl-Majíd traveled to ʻAkká to attain the presence of Baháʼuʼlláh, who addressed him as Abá Badíʻ (Father of Badíʻ). His spoken chronicle, as reported in *The Revelation of Baháʼuʼlláh* by Taherzadeh, contains the following dialogue beween Baháʼuʼlláh and himself:

One day I had the honour to be in the presence of the Blessed Beauty when He was talking about Badíʻ who had attained His presence, carried His Blessed Tablet to Ṭihrán [for Náṣiriʼd-Dín Sháh] and won the crown of martyrdom. As He was speaking, my tears were flowing profusely and my beard became wet. Baháʼuʼlláh turned to me and said "Abá Badíʻ! A person who has already spent three-quarters of his life should offer up the remainder in the path of God . . ." I asked "Is it possible that my beard which is now soaked in my tears may one day be dyed crimson with my blood?" The Blessed Beauty replied "God willing . . ."*

After returning to Khurásán, his native land, Abá Badíʻ continued attending the Baháʼí gatherings and serving the Cause with greater enthusiasm and devotion. This great zeal and his dedication to the Faith fanned the fire of hatred which was smoldering in the hearts of his enemies. These people, headed by the sister and the brother of Abá Badíʻ, reported his activities to their religious leaders. These reports and complaints provided an opportunity

---

* The words attributed to Baháʼuʼlláh are not necessarily His exact words. These are the recollections of Abá Badíʻ, but convey the sense of what He said.

for three of the leading mujtahids* to send a petition to the governor of Khurásán, the brother of the king, demanding the execution of Abá Badí'. But the governor was an amiable man and had no desire to harm this innocent person. Under the enormous pressure exerted by the clergy, however, he ordered the detention of Abá Badí', but did not pursue the matter any further. Then the mujtahids became impatient, wrote to the king, and enlisted his support for the elimination of Abá Badí'. The king directed the governor to release the victim only if he denied allegiance to the new Faith; otherwise, he should be subjected to the religious law. But the governor was extremely reluctant to shed the blood of a blameless old man. He did, therefore, his best to save Abá Badí''s life. It is reported that the governor sent, at different times, no less than twelve dignitaries of the province of Khurásán to persuade Abá Badí' to change his mind. None of them had any success with Abá Badí', whose heart was overflowing with the love of Bahá'u'lláh. Through one of the emissaries he sent a message to the governor saying that he could neither renounce nor dissimulate his Faith. Another one of the men reported that instead of paying attention to the advice of the governor, Abá Badí' was engaged in teaching him the Bahá'í Faith. At this point, the governor had no choice but to give in to the pressure and wishes of the clergy. He then reluctantly issued the execution order of Ḥájí 'Abdu'l-Majíd, Abá Badí', who was a tower of strength and a symbol of certitude and devotion. Here is an account, as told by Taherzadeh, of how Abá Badí''s glorious earthly life came to an end:

One day before his martyrdom, Abá Badí' asked a certain believer, Khadíjih Khánum, who used to visit him every day in jail and was a link between him and the believers, not to come again, for he knew that the next day was to be his last in this world. He had a dream that they brought a horse on which to take him away; he mounted the horse, but when he arrived at Maydán-i-Arg (a public square in Mashhad) he

---

* See footnote to Dream #31.

fell from the horse. He told <u>Kh</u>adíjih <u>Kh</u>ánum that this public square would be the scene of his martyrdom.

The following day, the jailer secretly informed the believers that the fateful hour had arrived and the execution would take place that day. The friends, grief-stricken, gathered in the House of Bábíyyih* praying and waiting for news. In the meantime a number of government officials, the executioners and a large crowd of people had gathered outside the prison. After a few hours, the old but imposing figure of Abá Badí' emerged from the prison. His radiant face and white beard gave him a dignified bearing, while the heavy chain around his frail neck made him the very picture of meekness and resignation. He was conducted amid the jeers and insults of a hostile crowd to the court of the Governor. On the way he faced the spectators and, beaming with joy, recited these two lines of a celebrated Persian poem:

> To God's pleasure we are resigned;
> A chained lion feels no shame.
> To my neck the Beloved's cord is tied;
> He leads me whither His will ordains.

. . . Abá Badí' was led by the executioners to Maydán-i-Arg where great crowds had gathered to watch him die. One of the friends pushed his way through the people, until he came close to him. There he pleaded with him to recant at the last moment, saying it would save his life and would do no harm to his Faith. In reply Abá Badí' recited this Persian poem:

> Set thy trap for another bird;
> This is the phoenix and it nests high.

---

* An historic house which was once the centre of great activities for the Bábís in Ma<u>sh</u>had, the capital city of the Province of <u>Kh</u>urásán. See Nabíl-i-A'ẓam, *The Dawn-Beakers*, p. 267.

The Governor, who was very reluctant to shed the blood of a holy and innocent man, hoped that the fierce scene of execution might frighten Abá Badí' and induce him to recant. Just as the execution was about to take place a special envoy from the Governor arrived at the scene and for the last time pleaded with him in vain to save his own life. But Abá Badí' was the embodiment of steadfastness in the Cause of God. Neither the clamour of the people, their insults and persecutions, nor the dreadful sight of the executioner, who stood dagger in hand beside him, were able to deter him from the path of God. . . . He stood serene and calm, unperturbed by the ferocity and brutality of his persecutors.

At last the officer in charge gave the signal and the executioner, dressed in red, stepped forward.[48]

# 49

In a series of memoirs, Munírih Khánum, relates briefly the story of her early life and the events prior and leading to her marriage with 'Abdu'l-Bahá. She was born into one of the most distinguished families of Isfahán. Several members of her family were involved in some of the major events of Bábí and Bahá'í history. Her father, Mírzá Muḥammad-'Alí, for example, had been a Shaykhí and had become a Bábí shortly after the Declaration of the Báb. He met the Báb in Isfahán and later participated in the conference of Badasht.* Munírih Khánum herself grew up during the critical period when the Bábí community was being transformed into the Bahá'í community. Isfahán, where she lived, was one of the most important Bahá'í communities in Iran, and her family was, in many ways, the pivot of that community. The following three accounts are taken from the book, *Munírih, Memoirs and Letters*. Munírih Khánum recounts:

Everyday at sunset, I would go onto the roof of the house to chant poetry and prayers until well into the evening. My mother would become vexed with me and would ask why I behaved in this way. Finally, one night I came down from the roof in a bad temper and found myself very depressed. That night I dreamed I was walking in a wilderness, and someone was following me. Suddenly he caught up with me, and I saw that he was riding a horse. He said, "Why are you afraid? Come, climb up behind me and I will take you wherever you want to go." He helped me mount and asked: "What is your desire?"

I said, "I beg God to give me two wings, so I can fly." The rider took hold of me and held me up. Suddenly, I realized that I had two wings and was flying. I flew for some time until I reached a vast arena full of people. I saw a high pulpit on which the Prophet Muḥammad stood.

---

* See Dreams #26 and #27.

All the prophets and messengers were seated there. At that moment, I turned into a dove. I flew up and settled in one of the niches on the pulpit. The Prophet placed a necklace around my neck and I flew away to unseen places that no words can describe. There I saw people in a state of prayer, among them my mother. I gave her the necklace and flew away again.

Then, I awoke. I was exhilarated and began to cry. My poor mother came to me to find out what was wrong. All that day I felt strange. After that, on most nights I would dream that I was soaring. And I was extremely happy because I knew that dreams of flying are good omens.[49]

# 50

Below is another account related by Munírih Khánum:

. . . Sayyid Mihdi Dahji* came to Isfahán at the instruction of the Ancient Beauty to proclaim the Faith. All the believers came to meet him, to inquire about news from the Holy Land, and to question him about the Beloved. Among them was Shamsu'd-Duha, a relative of the King of the Martyrs† and my aunt. She asked: "While you were in the holy Presence [of Bahá'u'lláh] did you ever hear Him speak of any girl He may have selected to marry the Master?" Sayyid Mihdi Dahiji replied: "I heard nothing about that. However, one day when the Blessed Beauty was in the outer rooms of the house, as He paced about He said, 'Áqá Sayyid Mihdi, last night I had a strange dream. I dreamt that the face of the beautiful girl in Tehran,‡ whose hand in marriage we have asked from our brother Mírzá Hasán for the Most Great Branch, gradually became darkened and indistinct. At the same time, another girl appeared with a luminous face and a luminous heart. I have chosen her for the Most Great Branch.' That is all I have heard."

When my aunt returned home and saw me she said, "I swear by the one true God, at the very moment when Áqá Sayyid Mihdi told this story, I felt that—without a shadow of a doubt—you are that girl! You will see!"

---

* He was a prominent Bahá'í who was given the title Ismu'lláhi'l-Mihdi, 'The Name of God, Mihdi' by Bahá'u'lláh. He later broke the Covenant.

† Mírzá Hasan, Munírih Khánum's cousin together with his brother Mírzá Husayn were martyred in Isfahán. Bahá'u'lláh conferred upon them the designations of the King of Martyrs and the Beloved of the Martyrs, respectively. See Dream #53.

‡ Sháh-Banu Khánum, the niece of Bahá'u'lláh, was intended to be 'Abdu'l-Bahá's wife. But her uncle, who was her guardian as well, Mírzá Rida-Quli, together with her aunt, a half-sister of Bahá'u'lláh, blocked the proposed marriage.

With tears in my eyes I said, "May God forgive me! How can I be worthy? I beg you not to say this again and not to mention it to anyone."

Not long after this, a Tablet arrived from the Holy Land in honor of the King of Martyrs. In it the Blessed Beauty said, "We have accounted you as one of our near ones and kindred." When my relative read this phrase, he immediately sent for all the members of the family and asked: "Have any of you sent a petition to the Blessed Beauty? What is this bounty? What are the glad tidings in this Tablet?"

We all replied that no one had written anything.

The King of the Martyrs said, "In that case, this Tablet must not be spread among the believers until its meaning becomes apparent."

Several months later, <u>Sh</u>ay<u>kh</u> Salmán* arrived in Iṣfahán from the Holy Land and told the King of Martyrs. "I carry glad tidings and untold bounties. Your cousin, the daughter of the late Mírzá Muḥammad-'Alí, is to accompany me to Mecca with the Muslim pilgrims going there, as though we too are making a pilgrimage to the Kaaba. You must make preparations for this journey until the usual time of Hajj, when we can set out and travel by way of <u>Sh</u>íráz and Búshihr. However, do not give out this news until two or three days before our departure."

When the time of Hajj arrived, Munírih <u>Kh</u>ánum accompanied by <u>Sh</u>ay<u>kh</u> Salmán, her brother, and a servant started her journey to 'Akká. Because of the limitation in the living quarters of the Holy Family her marriage to 'Abdu'l-Bahá could not take place until some five months after her arrival in 'Akká. Then 'Abbúd† annexed a room from his own adjoining house to the private quarters of the holy household. In March 1873, soon after this extension, the marriage of 'Abdu'l-Bahá and Munírih <u>Kh</u>ánum took place, in the presence of Bahá'u'lláh.[50]

---

* The believer who for forty years carried Tablets and letters back and forth between Bahá'u'lláh and the Bahá'ís of Iran. See 'Abdu'l-Bahá, *Memorials of the Faithful*, pp. 13–16.

† Ilyás 'Abbúd's house was next to Bahá'u'lláh's last residence in the city of 'Akká. This residence is known as the house of 'Abbúd, and is also the location in which the Most Holy Book (Aqdas) was revealed by Bahá'u'lláh.

# 51

On their way to ʿAkká, Munírih Khánum and her companions passed through the cities of Shíráz, Bushihr, Jeddah, Mecca, and Alexandria. While in Bushihr, she had a beautiful dream, which she later described in the following words:

> After our arrival in Bushihr from Shíráz, one afternoon we went to a caravanserai. As I had never seen the sea before, I immediately climbed onto the roof and saw a vast and limitless ocean. I thought to myself: I must travel across this sea, from one world to another. Thoughts of my family and friends, and many memories of my mother came to mind. I could not stop the tears from flowing . . . I came down from the roof in an indescribable condition—submerged in a sea of happiness, but sorrowful at my separation from my family and friends and my sisters. That night I felt very strange. Still fully dressed and wearing my full veil, I put my head on my saddle-bag and fell asleep.
>
> I dreamt that I was wandering in a vast wilderness. A pearl necklace that I was wearing suddenly broke and all the pearls fell to the ground. With a heavy heart, I started to pick them up. Then I suddenly saw that each pearl was growing until it became the size of an egg or even larger. Some had joined together. They sparkled and shone so much that they illuminated the wilderness. It was so beautiful and pleasing that the words of the Báb recorded in the Persian Bayán came to mind: "Endeavor ye, to present every unique and precious object to Him whom God shall make manifest." I told myself that it would be good to take these pearls and present them to the Blessed Beauty when I attained His presence. A container appeared, and I placed the pearls in it and lifted it onto my head.
>
> In a loud voice I called "O Thou whom God shall make manifest! O Thou whom God shall make manifest!" After proceeding for some time, I saw that a branch had grown out of the middle of the container.

It seemed to be guiding me to the Holy Land by alternately rising and prostrating. As it did so, a melodious voice could be heard coming from the branch, intoning, "Alláh-u-Akbar! Alláh-u-A'zam! Alláh-u-Abhá!" I joined in with this glorification and praise. My moans and exclamations in my sleep were so loud that my brother, Sayyid Yaḥyá, awoke and roused me saying, "Sister, sister, what has happened to you that you moan and cry out so much?"

I told him of my dream, but I could not describe it adequately. Right then and there, I wrote down all that had occurred in my dream and sent it to my mother in Isfahán.[51]

# 52

Mírzá Ashraf of Abadeh* was a radiant individual and a great Bahá'í teacher. Because of his teaching activities, he was arrested by Prince Zellu's-Sultan† and put in prison. In the *Bihjatu's-Sudur*, it is recorded:

A few days later the Prince invited a number of divines including Áqá Najafí (the Son of the Wolf)‡ to interrogate Mírzá Ashraf in his presence. With great eloquence and conviction, Ashraf in a loud voice, which could be heard outside the room, declared his beliefs and proved the validity of the Faith he had embraced. Confounded and utterly helpless to refute his arguments in support of the Faith, the divines used their usual weapon of denunciation. Áqá Najafí wrote Ashraf's death sentence and delivered it into the hands of the Prince who ordered his execution.

Shortly before his martyrdom, Mírzá Ashraf had a dream which he related to his friends, "In my dream I saw the Báb who was floating between the earth and the heaven. He motioned to me to go up to Him. I found strength in myself to fly upward. As I got up, my cloak fell off but I went up close to His Holiness. He said to me, 'Look.' I looked and saw that all the people of the world had gathered harmoniously together. Their faces were radiant and all of them were singing, in unison, the praises of the Greatest Name."

Mírzá Ashraf himself and all his Bahá'í friends interpreted his dream as a herald to the freedom of his soul from the cage of his physical form.[52]

---

* A town 397 miles south of Tihrán and 143 miles from Isfahán.

† Prince Mas'ud Mírzá, the Zillu's-Sultán, Násiri'd-Dín Sháh's eldest son, stigmatized by Bahá'u'lláh as "the Infernal Tree," He was a tyrannical man who, at one time, was a ruler over two-fifths of his father's kingdom.

‡ Shaykh Muhammad-Taqi, better known as Áqá Najafí, an inveterate enemy of the Faith and influential divine of Isfahán, to whom Bahá'u'lláh addressed His last outstanding Tablet, the *Epistle to the Son of the Wolf.*

# 53

There were two Bahá'í brothers who lived in Isfahán, Iran. Their names were Mírzá Muḥammad-Ḥusayn and Mírzá Muḥammad-Hasan. After their martyrdom, Bahá'u'lláh honored them with the appellations of the Beloved of Martyrs and the King of Martyrs, respectively. The two brothers, well known for their piety, kindness, and generosity, were beheaded in Isfahán in the year 1879. This heinous act was carried out at the instigation of two greedy and vicious divines: Mir Muḥammad-Ḥusayn whom Bahá'u'lláh called Raqsha (the She-Serpent) and Shaykh Muḥammad-Báqir stigmatized by Bahá'u'lláh as Dhi'b (the Wolf). The bodies of the two brothers, after having been exposed to the indignities heaped upon them by a shameless and degraded mob, were buried in the Takht-i Fulad cemetery.

In 1888 Edward G. Browne, the famous British Orientalist, was visiting Isfahán. In that city he found and befriended a Bahá'í whose name was Áqá Javad and whom Professor Browne calls *dallal*. In the company of Áqá Javad, Browne paid a visit to the graves of the two martyred brothers. He describes his visit to that blessed spot as follows:

> Next day, early in the afternoon, my friend the dallal came to conduct me to the tombs of the martyrs. After a walk of more than an hour in a blazing sun, we arrived at the vast cemetery called Takht-i-Fulad ("the Throne of Steel"). Threading our way through the wilderness of tombstones, my companion presently espied, and summoned to us, a poor grave-digger, also belonging to the persecuted sect, who accompanied us to a spot marked by two small mounds of stones and pebbles. Here we halted, and the dallal, turning to me, said, "These are the graves of the martyrs. No stone marks the spot, because the Musulmans destroyed those which we placed here, and, indeed, it is perhaps as well that they have almost forgotten the resting-places of those they slew, lest, in their fanaticism, they should yet further desecrate them. And now we will sit down for a while in this place, and I will tell you

how the death of these men was brought about. But first it is well that our friend should read the prayer appointed for the visitation of this holy spot."

The other thereupon produced a little book from under his cloak, and proceeded to read a prayer, partly in Arabic, partly in Persian. When this was concluded, we seated ourselves by the graves, and the dallal commenced his narrative.

"This," said he, pointing to the mound nearest to us, "is the tomb of Ḥájí Mírzá Hasan, whom we call Sultánu'sh-Shuhadá', 'the King of Martyrs,' and that yonder is the resting-place of his elder brother, Ḥájí Mírzá Ḥusayn, called Mahbúbu'sh-Shuhadá', 'the Beloved of Martyrs.' They were Siyyids by birth, and merchants by profession; yet neither their descent from the Prophet, nor their rare integrity in business transactions and liberality to the poor, which were universally acknowledged, served to protect them from the wicked schemes of their enemies . . . But we cannot mark the spot where they are buried with a stone, for when one was put up, the Musulmans, whose malignity towards us is unbounded, and who know very well that we pay visits to these graves in secret, overthrew it. Our friend here" (pointing to his companion) "was brought to believe by means of these martyrs. Was it not so?"

"Yes," answered the other, "some time after their death I saw in a dream vast crowds of people visiting a certain spot in the cemetery. I asked in my dream, 'Whose are these graves?' An answer came, 'Those of the "King of Martyrs" and the "Beloved of Martyrs."' Then I believed in that faith for which they had witnessed with their blood, seeing that it was accepted of God; and since then I visit them continually, and strive to keep them neat and orderly, and preserve the spot from oblivion by renewing the border of bricks and the heap of stones which is all that marks it."[53]

# 54

Siyyid Asadu'lláh-i-Qumí was a renowned teacher who attained the presence of Bahá'u'lláh, Who permitted him to reside permanently in 'Akká. He served the Cause for many years and was one of those who accompanied 'Abdu'l-Bahá in His European and American travels.

On one of his teaching trips, Siyyid Asadu'lláh-i-Qumí arrived in Arák.* In this city lived Mírzá Áqá <u>Kh</u>án,† an erudite and benevolent youth who was a devout Muslim. His father, being a liberal man, invited Siyyid Asadu'lláh to his home. Mírzá Áqá <u>Kh</u>án was displeased with this invitation and resented the idea of entertaining a Bahá'í in their home. At the same time, he was confident that he could easily overwhelm the Bahá'í teacher and put an end to all that nonsense. So, during the discussion sessions with Siyyid Asadu'lláh, he became quite aggressive and proceeded with verbal assault. But the Siyyid managed to calm him down through his charm and loving kindness. Then Mírzá Áqá <u>Kh</u>án began to listen to the words of the Bahá'í teacher and the proofs he presented on the authenticity of the station of Bahá'u'lláh. Under the influence of the convincing arguments and the Siyyid's radiant spirit, Mírzá Áqá <u>Kh</u>án and his cousin both accepted the Faith. Soon Mírzá Áqá <u>Kh</u>án became a distinguished Bahá'í and very active in teaching and in serving the Cause. Financially, however, he was facing difficulties and many challenges. Then he had a dream that profoundly affected his living conditions. This dream is related by Taherzadeh in *The Revelation of Bahá'u'lláh* as follows:

---

* A city of west-central Iran about 183 miles from Tihrán. Previously, it was known as Sultanabad.

† He was the grandson of Mírzá Abu'l-Qasim Farahani, entitled Qá'im Maqám, who was a contemporary of Bahá'u'lláh's father and his faithful friend. He was the Prime Minister of Iran from 1821 until 1835 when he was killed by the order of Muḥammad <u>Sh</u>áh.

Bahá'u'lláh appeared to him, pointed to a hill nearby, and directed him to dig out some valuable relics which were buried on the side of the hill. Believing his dream to be true, Mírzá Áqá Khán carried out the excavation and recovered a great quantity of priceless relics and jewels. He thus became one of the richest men in Arák and the most influential of its residents. Throughout his long years of life he used his enormous wealth and influence to further the interests of the Cause he loved and served so well. Although he was wealthy, he lived a very simple life. He was a tower of strength for the believers and a guide and refuge for the downtrodden and the needy. His generosity, magnanimity and care for the welfare of people earned him the love and respect of the public in general and the Bahá'ís in particular.

In a Tablet addressed to him 'Abdu'l-Bahá states that his grandfather, Qá'im-Maqám, is rejoicing in the Abhá Kingdom, for God has enabled his grandson to become a sign of guidance to the people, a bearer of the standard of the Kingdom and a manifestation of the bounties of heaven.[54]

# 55

Mírzá Yusuf Khan-i Vujdani was a great Bahá'í teacher whose life spanned the ministries of Bahá'u'lláh, 'Abdu'l-Bahá, and Shoghi Effendi. From his mother's side, he was a grandson of Fath-'Alí <u>Sh</u>áh.* His original name was Kalb-'Alí, which was changed to Yusuf (Joseph) by 'Abdu'l-Bahá when Yusuf had the bounty of being in His presence in the Holy Land. Earlier in his life, he traversed the valley of search with much patience and suffering. By the grace of the Almighty, he eventually found the city of his beloved. He became one of the most active and learned Bahá'ís of his time, and for a period he tutored the Branches† in the Mansion.

The following is taken from his own written account about his conversion to the Bahá'í Faith in Malayer.‡ It should be mentioned here that prior to his convincing dream, Vujdani had heard of the Bahá'í Faith and had a few acquaintances among the Bahá'ís. Vujdani recounts:

I had a dream in which I saw myself standing in the middle of a vast, pleasant and serene plain. It was a bright and peaceful morning. From the heavens above, a heart-rending voice repeating, "He, in truth, hath manifested Him who is the Dayspring of Revelation, Who conversed on Sinai" was penetrating my ears and my very soul. Buoyed by a feeling of joy and excitement, I joined the chorus and recited the verse with a pleasant and loud voice. I grew quite conscious of the verse and after repeating it several times I woke up, still uttering the words. . . . Later on that day, Mr. Mowzoon§ came to see me. After

---

* He was the second Qájár king of Iran who ruled from 1797 to 1834.
† A designation used by Bahá'u'lláh to refer to His male descendants.
‡ A city in western Iran about 240 miles west of Tihrán.
§ He was a renowned Bahá'í teacher and a great poet from Malayer. His original name was Husayn-Qulí Mírzá. Bahá'u'lláh honored him with more than one hundred Tablets in which He addressed him as *Mowzoon*.

96 | *Dreams of Destiny*

the exchange of greetings, I requested his guidance for the choice of a dhikr.* He then informed me that the Sufi tradition of dhikr was not practiced in the Bahá'í Faith and that it was required of every Bahá'í to recite the Greatest Name 95 times a day. Further, he told me that he had with him a copy of one of the Bahá'í Obligatory Prayers. I was greatly surprised to hear that there were new obligatory prayers and that the ordinances of the Qur'án had been supplanted. At any rate, I asked him for the copy of the prayer. As I looked at that blessed page and saw what the Ancient Beauty had revealed, I was totally overcome by a sense of awe and attraction. "He, in truth, hath manifested Him Who is the Dayspring of Revelation, Who conversed on Sinai,"†—the same verse of my dream.[56]

---

* *Remembrance, invocation, praise and glorification of God.* In Sufism, an exercise in which the names of God are chanted or mentioned repeatedly.

† The third sentence in the Medium Obligatory Prayer.

# 56

Áqá Sha<u>ykh</u> Haydar, known as *Mu'allim* (teacher), was a great soul who became a believer at the beginning of 'Abdu'l-Bahá's ministry. He was by birth a Tatar* who throughout his Bahá'í life was occupied with teaching the children and the youth. As a young man, he left Tatarstan and went to Bukhara† to pursue his religious studies. In Bukhara, he studied hard and soon became a scholar in the fields of literature and jurisprudence. Despite his great accomplishments and his intimate association with the scholars and the leading theologians, his heart felt restless, and he was not content. He could not find that reality for which he was searching. He was not satisfied with the commentaries written on the Qur'án and found the allegorical verses of that Holy Book very puzzling. It was at such a time that the <u>Shaykh</u> had a strange dream that added to his perplexity and confoundment.

One night in a dream, he saw himself in a heavenly garden that had no boundaries. In this garden, there were many expansive avenues that were lux-uriously lined with very tall trees. The grounds were covered with beautiful plants and flowers, and the water that was flowing in the graceful rivers was as pure as crystal. There was placed, in one of the avenues, a table of normal height and width but of an infinite length. No one could see either the begin-ning or the end of this table upon which were placed all kinds of exquisite food, drinks, and fruits. There were chairs of high quality arranged on both sides of this table. The dining wares were royally arranged on the table, but the chairs were empty, except for a few. These few chairs were all occupied by individuals of different races and nationalities. The number of the people sitting at the table was so few that it seemed that only two chairs out of every few thousands were occupied. These few people were helping themselves to

---

* Also, Tartar, a member of a group of Turkic people inhabiting primarily the autonomous Republic of Tatarstan in west-central Russia, parts of Siberia and Central Asia. The capital of Tatarstan is Kazan.

† An ancient city in Uzbekistan.

all those provisions, and when a person could not reach a certain item on the table, soon would appear a hand, from out of nowhere, and would give the desired item to that individual. In his dream, the Shaykh was greatly puzzled at the sight of that strange and wonderful setting. He was wondering about the place, about all those provisions, and about the power behind that hand. In the midst of his bewilderment, he heard a voice. He was certain that the voice belonged to the same person whose hand he had previously seen. The voice uttered these words, "Behold, how the people of the world are heedless. They cannot distinguish between the things that are heavenly and bring blessing to them and the things that are pernicious and cause them misery and ruin. Through the grace of God, all these victuals are prepared for them, and all have been invited, but none come forward. All of them have deprived themselves of these heavenly provisions." After this dream, the Shaykh's outlook on life changed. He knew that it was a spiritual and meaningful dream and that its significance would be divulged in due course. Leaving Bukhara behind, the Shaykh traveled to different cities in Iran, including Tihrán, where he tarried a while and pursued his studies in fields that were quite new to him. Eventually he arrived at Sari,* where he settled down and resumed his teaching career. It was in this city where a learned Bahá'í teacher befriended the Shaykh and gave him, discreetly, the Kitáb-i Íqán.† This book to him was like a glass of cool water in the hands of a thirsty person. In the privacy of his room and in the stillness of the night, he read the Book of Certitude several times. Soon after partaking of this heavenly food, he accepted the mission of Bahá'u'lláh and became one of the most intrepid teachers of His Cause. Subsequently, he moved to Tihrán where he resumed his profession as a teacher. At the same time, he was chosen as a tutor of the children at the royal court of Mozaffaru'd-Din Sháh.‡ It was in this capacity that the Shaykh could guide one of the ladies of the royal family to the Bahá'í Faith.§56

---

* See footnote to Dream # 23.
† Also called the Book of Certitude, is one of the most important books of Bahá'u'lláh.
‡ The fifth king of the Qájár dynasty who ruled Iran from May 1896 to January 1907.
§ See the following account.

# 57

Áqá <u>Sh</u>ay<u>kh</u> Haydar, known as *Mu'allim* (teacher), was employed as a tutor in the court of Mozaffaru'd-Din <u>Sh</u>áh in Iran. There, he was teaching mainly the Qur'án and its commentaries to his students. At the same time, he was incorporating into his presentations some of the spiritual concepts and progressive ideas that he had learned from the Bahá'í writings. As a result of this approach, his students found his expositions and comments gratifying and of special quality. And since he was a man of high moral conduct, the princesses of the court looked upon him as a saint and showed him much respect and consideration.

One night, one of the princesses had a dream. In her dream, she found herself totally lost in an unfamiliar part of the city. She walked for many hours in the crooked, narrow, and scary lanes until it became dark. Then she saw some thieves and murderers who, emerging from their covered hideouts, were looking for their next victim. She was a woman of great beauty and was wearing elegant and expensive clothing and jewelry. Her realization of the potential and imminent danger frightened her to death. Helplessly, she was running here and there to find an escape. But, to her utter dismay, she ended up in a dead-end lane where she saw only a single window that was located about three feet above the ground. There were no normal entry doors to any of the houses on this lane. Realizing that escape was impossible, her pounding heart lost all traces of hope. At this point of total despair and anguish, she began praying earnestly and asking God to come to her deliverance. Suddenly the door to that little window was opened and a very affectionate man invited her to enter. The kindly tone of the man's voice imparted confidence in her heart and she entered through the window. Then she saw the place to be a vast and beautiful garden. The man assured her that she had arrived in a safe place and asked her to follow him to see the owner of the garden. She followed him and soon they came to a building. They climbed the stairs and entered a room in which was seated, with much dignity, a venerable man. As soon as the princess saw this man she bowed to him and went forward and threw herself at his feet to kiss them. But that honorable man raised her tenderly and allowed her to be seated. Then he said to her, "Relax and do not be troubled, no harm will come to you here. This place is a haven for the distraught and an asylum for the orphans and the forsaken." Sheer joy and exaltation woke her up from this dream, which was then vividly imprinted in her memory.

At her next meeting with the <u>Shaykh</u>, the princess related her dream and asked him for its interpretation. He asked her if she remembered the features of that venerable man. The princess responded by saying that all the details were engraved in her eyes. The <u>Shaykh</u> wanted her to acquaint him with those features, and the princess described some. The <u>Shaykh</u> said nothing more on that day. At the next session, however, he showed her, in private, a picture of 'Abdu'l-Bahá and asked her if she knew that face. She immediately grabbed the picture and, with much amazement, said, "This is Him, He is that very venerable man of my dream. My life may be a sacrifice to Him. He is my deliverer, the eyes are the same and the attire is exactly the same. He is my Master; please tell me who He is." This gave the <u>Shaykh</u> the opportunity to acquaint the princess with the Bahá'í Faith. Before long, she embraced the cause of God with much joy and happiness. Then gradually and with grace and wisdom, she introduced several other members of the royal family to the <u>Shaykh</u>. The result was the acceptance of the Faith by some of them and the introduction of the Cause into that royal establishment.[57]

# 58

Mullá Bahram was the first Zoroastrian who accepted the Bahá'í Faith in Yazd.* After his conversion, he rose up with much dedication to acquaint his co-religionists with the message of Bahá'u'lláh. It was due to his sustained and devoted efforts that a large number of the Zoroastrians accepted the Faith. His wife, however, was very unhappy that her husband had left the religion of their forefathers. She remained hostile to the Bahá'í Faith and to him and tried to obstruct his efforts. 'Abdu'l-Bahá conferred upon this dedicated man, Mullá Bahram, the title of *Akhtar-i-Khavari*, which means *Star of the East*.

One night, Mullá Bahram saw two Siyyids in his dream. They entered his house and told him that they were Nayyir and Sina.† On the following day he went to his farm to irrigate it. On the same day, Nayyir and Sina arrived at Mihdi-Abad,‡ the village where Mullá Bahram resided. Because of the persecutions, the two brothers had fled from Isfahán to Yazd, from where they had to flee again for the same reason. They managed to find the house of Mullá Bahram and knocked at the door. His wife opened the door and saw two green-turbaned strangers. She was a bit frightened and quickly closed the door, saying, "This is not Mullá Bahram's house." Crestfallen, Nayyir and Sina started walking away from that house. On the road they saw Mullá Bahram, who was returning home. As soon as his eyes fell on the faces and attires of the two brothers, he recognized them as the same two in his dream. He approached and asked them if they were Nayyir and Sina. They confirmed that they were and asked him, "Are you Mullá Bahram?" After answering positively, he embraced and welcomed the brothers to Mihdi-Abad and took them to his home.[58]

---

* Yazd is one of the provinces of Iran located in the center of the country. The city of Yazd, some 175 miles southwest of Iṣfahán, is its provincial capital.

† Mullá Bahram had probably heard the names of the two famous Bahá'í brothers.

‡ A village in Yazd province, some 68 miles SW of Yazd city.

# 59

Siyyid Muḥammad and Siyyid Isma'il, better known by their adopted names of Nayyir and Sina, respectively, were two brothers from Sidih of Isfahán. Both brothers were learned individuals who were quite active in the promotion of the Cause of God. For this purpose, they traveled extensively in Iran and suffered much. The two brothers were also gifted poets who used their talent in the praise and service of their Faith.

During one of their travel-teaching trips, Nayyir and Sina arrived in Arák. One afternoon, while they were taking a nap to rest their wearied bodies, Nayyir had a dream. After they woke up, he said to Sina, "Brother, I dreamed that someone was knocking at the door. When I opened the door I saw that it was Mírzá Abu'l-Faḍl* of Gulpáygán. I invited him in and brought him into this very room." Sina started interpreting his brother's dream when they heard a knock at the door. Nayyir jumped up and opened the door; it was Mírzá Abu'l-Faḍl. He guided Mírzá to the same room. When the eyes of the two brothers next met, they burst into a laughter that could not be stopped. This puzzled Mírzá Abu'l-Faḍl, who inquired about the reason behind the laughter. But they had a hard time stopping their laughter. Eventually they managed to tell him the cause of their laughter. This made Mírzá Abu'l-Faḍl happy and welcomed.[59]

---

* The great Bahá'í scholar and one of the Apostles of Bahá'u'lláh.

# 60

In one of his trips in the middle of the winter, Sina had one of his sons with him and was going from village to village to teach the Faith and to visit the Bahá'ís. In one dark and rainy night, he became quite ill and paralyzed. His son and a guide turned back and took him to the nearest village that they had passed earlier. They had not entered this village because they feared a hostile reception. In her book *Fire on the Mountaintop*, Gloria Faizi has written:

To their surprise, they were received very kindly and taken into a house where a man and several women immediately kindled a large fire and started to dry their clothes. The womenfolk showed great concern over Sina who lay unconscious all this while and one old woman, in particular, could not dry her tears as she sat beside the helpless patient. It seemed like a miracle when, halfway through the night, Sina began to recover from his illness and found that he could use his tongue again. The first words he uttered were in praise and gratitude to God that he had once more been permitted to suffer hardship in the path of service to His Cause. Then he turned to the old woman who had kept faithful watch by his bedside and who now seemed eager to talk to him, but he could not understand what she said as she spoke in a colloquial dialect. In the morning, the woman brought a translator who explained to Sina that she had dreamed of him and his son three nights before. She had seen him lying there unconscious in her dream, just as she had now seen him in reality. "Who are you?" she enquired of Sina, "and what are you doing in this forest?" He told her that he had come to see a friend in the next village. His friend and fellow believer proved to be the old woman's grandson and, after a little more conversation, Sina found out that the woman herself was a Bahá'í, as was every inhabitant of the village in which they were staying! All the men of the village, with the exception of one, were out farming on the hills some distance away while the women stayed behind to do the work at home.[60]

# 61

Áqá Mírzá Ḥusayn was a steadfast and tested Bahá'í in Zanján. His brother, Mullá Muḥammad, was a religious leader who was very antagonistic toward the Bahá'í Faith. One day, this brother told Áqá Mírzá Ḥusayn that he had an ominous dream. In his dream he had seen a great and bloody flood descending from the mountainside, destroying and washing away several houses, including the one belonging to Áqá Mírzá Ḥusayn. He went on by saying: "Brother, you know that what I see in my dreams usually come to pass in the real life. Please stay away from your Bábí friends so that you would not be affected by a likely disaster." The Bahá'í brother responded by affirming his belief in the eventual triumph of the Cause of God. This response angered Mullá Muḥammad, who left the room with a grim face. At about the same time, the wife of Mr. Varqá had a dream which was very similar to that of the mullá.

Within a very short time of these two dreams, Mr. Varqá,* his twelve-year-old son (Rúhu'lláh), Áqá Mírzá Ḥusayn, and Ḥájí Imán (Varqá's father-in-law) were arrested by the order of the governor of Zanján. They were kept incarcerated for some two weeks in that city, after which they were dispatched to Tihrán under appalling conditions. In Tihrán they were imprisoned and put under heavy chains. This imprisonment proved to be the last one for Varqá and Rúhu'lláh. After being kept in the prison for some time, both of them were savagely murdered by the fiendish Hajibu'd-Dawlih, the officer in charge of the prison. The lives of the other two prisoners were, however, spared providentially. One of these two, Áqá Mírzá Ḥusayn, has left to posterity the circumstances related to the martyrdom of Varqá and Rúhu'lláh.[61]

---

* See Dream # 45.

# 62

The brutal murder of saintly Varqa and his illustrious son plunged Áqá Mírzá Ḥusayn into a sea of sorrow and grief. He became extremely agitated and confused. The whole night he could not sleep, and his tears were flowing constantly. Then he became exhausted, fell asleep, and had a dream. In his dream, Rúhu'lláh, with a bright and smiling face, approached him and said, "Áqá Mírzá Ḥusayn, did you see how I sat on the neck of the emperor?" Before his martyrdom, Rúhu'lláh's constant source of pride were the words of 'Abdu'l-Bahá. When he was about to leave His presence for the last time, 'Abdu'l-Bahá had put His hand on Rúhu'lláh's shoulder and had said, "Should it be the will of God, He would seat Rúhu'lláh on the neck of the emperor to proclaim His Cause."[62]

# 63

'Abdu'l-Bahá was the eldest son of Bahá'u'lláh, the Founder of the Bahá'í Faith. From earliest childhood, He shared His father's sufferings and banishments. His given name was 'Abbas Effendi, and took as His title *'Abdu'l-Bahá*, the *servant of Bahá*. Bahá'u'lláh appointed Him as the Center of His Covenant and as the one authorized to interpret the Bahá'í teachings and its sacred writings. After His release from the prison in 1908, 'Abdu'l-Bahá set out on a series of journeys that, from 1911 to 1913, took Him to Europe and America, where He proclaimed Bahá'u'lláh's message of unity and social justice to many public audiences.

Early on during the ministry of 'Abdu'l-Bahá, Siyyid Asadu'lláh-i-Qumí,* who was then in 'Akká, had a dream: in his dream, Bahá'u'lláh placed a few Tablets inside some envelopes, wrote on them in red ink, handed the envelopes to Siyyid Asadu'lláh, and directed him to proceed to Persia. In the morning, the Siyyid recounted his dream to 'Abdu'l-Bahá and asked permission to leave for Persia. 'Abdu'l-Bahá warned him that on this journey he would be severely persecuted in a special manner. This prophecy was fulfilled when Siyyid Asadu'lláh reached the city of Ardabíl in the province of Ádhirbáyján. A few of the clergy became aware of his teaching activities in the city and plotted to take his life. One day, he was conducted to a place where several men surrounded him and beat him so severely that they thought he was dead. They dragged his body into a disused stable. After some time, he regained consciousness but was taken into prison by the order of the governor. Later he was sent to the prison of Tabríz, in which he languished for a few days. Eventually orders arrived that he should be sent to Tihrán under escort. However, instead of taking him to a prison there, the prime minister (Amínu's-Sultán) gave instructions that the Siyyid should be brought to his own home, where he was received with kindness and consideration.

---

* See dream #54.

On his way to Tihrán, while escorted by the soldiers, Siyyid Asadu'lláh recalled the words of Bahá'u'lláh a few years earlier when on a certain occasion he had attained His presence in the Mansion of Mazra'ih in AH 1306 (AD 1888–89). He said to him, "Asadu'lláh, I want to send you to visit Násiri'd-Dín Sháh, but remember that he does not kill Bahá'ís any more. Do you wish to go?"* And Siyyid Asadu'lláh bowed as a sign of his submission to his Lord. Now he was a prisoner on his way to the capital and he knew that somehow he was going to meet the Sovereign. 'Abdu'l-Bahá writes:† "Amínu's-Sultán came to the prisoner's assistance and, in his own office, provided Asadu'lláh with a sanctuary. One day when the Prime Minister was ill, Násiri'd-Dín Sháh arrived to visit him. The Minister then explained the situation, and lavished praise upon his captive; so much so that the Sháh, as he left, showed great kindness to Asadu'lláh, and spoke words of consolation. This, when at an earlier time, the captive would have been strung up at once to adorn some gallows-tree and shot down with a gun."[63]

---

* These are not to be taken as the exact words of Bahá'u'lláh.
† 'Abdu'l-Bahá, *Memorials of the Faithful*, p. 137.

# 64

May Ellis Bolles (1870–1940) was a well-known early American Bahá'í and teacher of the Faith. She learned of the Faith in Paris when the first American pilgrims arrived there on their way to 'Akká. May joined the party, arriving in the Holy Land in February, 1899. This marked her acceptance of the Faith. When she returned to Paris, she formed the first Bahá'í group in Europe. She was very successful in her teaching activities, and many became familiar with the Faith and accepted it through her efforts. In 1902, she married William Sutherland Maxwell and moved with him to Montreal, where their home became a focus of teaching. They had one daughter, Mary, the future wife of Shoghi Effendi. May traveled widely for the Faith and was named a martyr by Shoghi Effendi after she passed away in her pioneering post, Buenos Aires, in 1940. "Mary Bolles was a woman of rare spiritual sensitivity. At the age of eleven she had had a dream in which she experienced a flash of light so bright that it blinded her for a day. During another dream, in 1895, she saw the earth from space; one word was written on the earth's surface, but the only letters of the word she could read were B and H.* At another time she experienced a vision of a man, clothed in Eastern garb, who beckoned her from across the Mediterranean."[64]

---

\* In Arabic and Persian, these are the first two letters of the word *Bahá*.

# 65

Násiri'd-Dín Sháh was the fourth Qájár king who ruled Iran from 1848 to 1896. During his reign, the Báb was martyred in Tabriz and Bahá'u'lláh was imprisoned in Iran and subsequently banished from that country, His native land. This king caused numerous deaths and untold suffering among the followers of the Báb and Bahá'u'lláh. He was stigmatized by Bahá'u'lláh as the "Prince of Oppressors," and to him Bahá'u'lláh revealed a Tablet that is the lengthiest epistle to any single sovereign.

Just a few nights before his golden jubilee, Násiri'd-Dín Sháh had a dream. In his dream, he saw the angels of wrath and torment bringing down a fiery coffin in which they purposed to place him. He woke up with a loud scream. Members of his family advised him not to sleep alone. Soon he went back to sleep and dreamed a second time. In this dream, Mírzá Taqí Khán Amír-i-Kabír,* with bloodshot eyes, appeared to him. He told Násiri'd-Dín Sháh that, on the following day, both the country and its inhabitants would be relieved from his tyranny. At the same time, the Sháh's wife woke up with a loud shriek. She told her husband that in her dream, she saw all the roofs of the palace come down upon them. That night the Sháh could not sleep any more. In the dead of the night he walked to the house of Mullá Aly-i Kaní† and related his dreams to him. The mujtahid's interpretation failed to calm Násiri'd-Dín Sháh. From that house, he rode his carriage to the Shrine of Sháh 'Abdu'l-Azim,‡ where he was killed by the bullet of an assassin.[65]

---

* The despotic prime minister of Násiri'd-Dín Shah who ordered the execution of the Báb.

† Mujtahid of Tihrán, the highest religious personality at that time and a fierce enemy of the Faith.

‡ The resting place of Abdu'llah Ibn-i-'Alí, a descendant of the Imám Hassan, the second Imám of Shí'ah Muslims.

# 66

Charles Greenleaf and his wife Elizabeth Greenleaf, were among the earliest American Bahá'ís. Both were quite active Bahá'ís and brought some great souls into the Faith through their teachings and steadfastness. Charles was a friend of Thornton Chase, the first American Bahá'í. It was Mr. Chase who introduced Charles Greenleaf to the Faith of Bahá'u'lláh. In 1907, in a Tablet addressed to Charles, 'Abdu'l-Bahá praised him and his wife for their services to the Cause: ". . . O thou who art firm in the Covenant! Thy services and those of thy revered wife are acceptable in the Kingdom of Abhá, for ye have made your home a nest for the birds of God, and have engaged in teaching the Cause of God. Ye are truthful gardeners of the Garden of God, and two agreeable servants of the Holy Threshold . . ."* Shoghi Effendi designated Charles Greenleaf as one of the Disciples of 'Abdu'l-Bahá.†

The Greenleafs were both students of Dr. Ibrahim Khayru'lláh who was the first Bahá'í from the Middle East to bring the message of Bahá'u'lláh to the United States of America. Mr. Greenleaf was a Baptist and had a deep and orthodox faith in Jesus Christ. Robert Stockman writes, "As such, Charles found the teacher's conclusions about the Bible, in spite of their logic, to be quite disconcerting, and acceptance of them came slowly. A nagging fear that he was being disloyal to Jesus persisted for a long time. He was finally convinced by a remarkable dream he had one night. In the dream he was in an oriental room. A figure with a face like that of Jesus Christ, as He was often depicted in paintings, sat on the couch opposite. As the figure rose and came toward him, Charles realized that the figure was not Jesus as He had first appeared on the earth. He was the Promised One. Charles awoke with the realization that Christ had returned."[66]

---

\* *Bahá'í World,* Volume 9, p. 608.

† Nineteen American and European individuals who were outstanding Bahá'ís during the ministry of 'Abdu'l-Bahá.

## 67

Mrs. Greenleaf was very knowledgeable in the Faith and was also quite effective in her teaching efforts. For a short time, she was a member of the National Spiritual Assembly of the Bahá'ís of the United States and Canada.* Upon her death in 1941, the Guardian sent the following cable: "Share deep grief of bereaved community at passing of Elizabeth Greenleaf beloved handmaid of Bahá'u'lláh. Her radiant spirit, staunch loyalty, noble character, effective teaching method were distinguishing features of her consecrated life . . ."†

Like her husband, Elizabeth Greenleaf also had a dream that was even more remarkable than that of her husband. This dream is reported in *The Bahá'í Faith in America* by Robert Stockman:

> In it she was in a room in an Asian country; Persian rugs lay on the floor, and low divans ran along all four walls. A magnificent, majestic figure sat on one divan, His face veiled by the brilliant light radiating from it. People bowed before Him. Seated on another divan was an equally glorious figure, but with a face she could see; it was filled with wisdom, compassion, love. On this second figure's forehead was written the word *Aqa*. When Elizabeth told the teacher of the class about her dream, he became excited and told her she was truly one of the chosen. The first figure, he explained, was "the Manifestation," Bahá'u'lláh, the return of the Father and God's latest Messenger to humanity, while the second was His son, the Christ‡ who was now alive on the earth, known as 'Abdu'l-Bahá and called by His followers "Aqa" or "the Master."[67]

---

* There was one National Spiritual Assembly for both countries until 1948 when a separate Assembly was established for Canada.

† Shoghi Effendi, *Messages to America*, p. 48.

‡ Bahá'ís do not equate 'Abdu'l-Bahá with Christ, although His actions and demeanor were quite similar to those of Christ.

# 68

Ibrahim Khayru'lláh, the teacher of the Greenleafs, was a charismatic man who became quite successful in his teaching activities during his first few years in America. He won many converts to the Faith, but soon he became conceited and began craving leadership. He tried to turn the young American Bahá'í community away from 'Abdu'l-Bahá, the appointed Center of Bahá'u'lláh's Covenant. He conceived the idea of writing a flattering letter to 'Abdu'l-Bahá and inviting the Bahá'ís to join in signing it. This petition contained the request that Khayru'lláh would be the head of the Faith in the West, while 'Abdu'l-Bahá would be the Head of the Faith in the East. Many of the believers who signed this petition followed Khayru'lláh into the wilderness. Two steadfast believers, who did not, were Elizabeth and Charles Greenleaf. Brent Poirier writes:

> Mrs. Greenleaf had decided not to sign the letter, though she could not explain why. Her husband disagreed, and this became a source of distance between them. One night Mrs. Greenleaf had a dream, and in this dream she was instructed to tell her husband, "Watch out for the white ram!" She had no idea what this meant. The next evening was the occasion of the meeting in which everyone was supposed to sign the petition. As her husband Charles was about to leave the house to attend the meeting, Elizabeth blurted out, "Watch out for the white ram!" Charles was startled, and his face turned pale. "What do you mean by this?" She said she did not know; only that she was told to warn him. He was very unsettled, and sat down to collect himself. He then recounted a recurring dream he had had about a white ram. He was walking through a beautiful meadow and he came to a deep chasm with rocks at the bottom. There was a narrow footbridge over the chasm, and as he approached it, a white ram appeared. The ram motioned that he should cross the bridge. However, he knew that if he attempted it, the ram would push him into the chasm. Then, as he gazed at the ram,

he said, "I saw that it had the eyes of our teacher, Ibrahim Khayrullah!" Mr. and Mrs. Greenleaf remained faithful to the Covenant to the end of their lives.[68]

# 69

Mullá 'Alí-Jan was a native of Mázindarán and was well-versed in the Qur'án and the traditions of Islám. The traditions extolling the merits of 'Akká were, however, quite puzzling to him. No one could explain them satisfactorily, until he became acquainted with a well-known Bahá'í, whose explanations satisfied him. After embracing the Cause of God, he became a ball of fire and began teaching people with much enthusiasm. He brought a great number of people from different villages under the banner of Bahá'u'lláh. Then the divines rose up against him and clamored for his death. He was conducted under appalling conditions to Tihrán, where he was brutally murdered. In the Epistle to the Son of the Wolf, Bahá'u'lláh says, "Meditate on the splendor and glory which the light of renunciation, shining from the upper chamber of the heart of Mullá 'Alí-Ján, hath shed."*

'Alawiyyih Khanum, the wife of the martyred 'Ali-Jan, was only twenty-three when she lost her husband. She never married again and spent the rest of her earthly life in teaching and serving the Cause of God. After the ascension of Bahá'u'lláh, she made a pilgrimage to the Holy Land and had the honor of attending the presence of 'Abdu'l-Bahá.

One day 'Abdu'l-Bahá related the following story to the friends who were gathered around Him:

> 'Alawiyyih Khánum, the wife of the martyr Mullá 'Alí Jan-i-Shahid,† had a dream. She related it to Jamál-i-Burujirdi.‡ She told him that in her dream Jamál-i-Mubárak (the Blessed Beauty) had come to visit her and had blessed her. Jamál said, "Your dream was a true one—I have

---

* Bahá'u'lláh, Epistle to the Son of the Wolf, p. 73.

† *Shahid* means *martyr.*

‡ For many years during Bahá'u'lláh's ministry, he was foremost among the teachers of the Faith in Iran, and his fame had spread throughout the community, but later, during the ministry of 'Abdu'l-Bahá, he broke the Covenant.

come here and I like you."* It would have been appropriate if she had done to Jamál what the princess did to that clumsy fellow. The princess had fallen in love with Mírzá 'Alí Khán-i-Núrí. One day she heard that a guest had arrived in the room. Thinking that the guest was none other than Mírzá 'Alí Khán-i-Núrí, she took a light and entered the room where she found a coarse and ugly man. She raised . . . both hands and began hitting the man on the head until his hat fell apart. All the while she was screaming, "Are you Mírzá 'Alí Khán-i-Núrí? Are you Mírzá 'Alí Khán-i-Núrí? You poor devil, are you Mírzá 'Alí Khán-i-Núrí?"[69]

---

* This conceited and arrogant man played on the similarity of Bahá'u'lláh's title, Jamál-i-Mubárak, to his own name, Jamál.

# 70

Ḥájí Maḥmúd Qassabchi was a dedicated Baháʼí from Iraq. During His ministry, ʻAbduʼl-Bahá commissioned him to attend to the much-needed repairs of the house of Baháʼuʼlláh in Baghdád. Ḥájí Maḥmúd was also the individual whose generous contributions made it possible for Shoghi Effendi to carry out the task of adding three additional rooms to the Báb's sepulcher. This addition changed the oblong shape of the edifice to a perfect square. Upon this square building was later erected the majestic superstructure that today graces the Shrine of the Báb on Mount Carmel. As a sign of his gratitude, Shoghi Effendi named a door on the eastern side of the Shrine after this devoted and generous Baháʼí.

One day, while he was in Baghdád, Mr. Abuʼl-Qasim Faizi, the Hand of the Cause of God, visited Ḥájí Maḥmúd Qassabchi. During the course of their conversation, Mr. Faizi mentioned that he considered the task of repairing the Most Great House to be a wonderful blessing. Then he asked Ḥájí Maḥmúd if he had any awareness, clue, or dream concerning this bounty, beforehand. Ḥájí said, "Yes, one night in my dream I saw that there was a large and noisy crowd on the roof of the House of Baháʼuʼlláh. I looked up and saw that there was a silk handkerchief suspended up in the air. All the people on the roof were jumping up and down to grab that handkerchief. I found myself to be longing for it too. So I stretched my hand up and, without any struggle, the handkerchief alighted on my hand and I put it in my pocket. It was not long after this dream that ʻAbduʼl-Bahá honored me with the task of repairing the Blessed House."[70]

# 71

Ḥájí Mullá 'Alí-Akbar-i-Shahmírzádí, better known as Ḥájí Ákhúnd, was one of the Hands of the Cause of God and an Apostle of Bahá'u'lláh. He encountered the Bábís at the age of nineteen and was, soon afterwards, converted to the Bábí Faith. Because of this conversion, he was rejected by his peer groups and persecuted by the religious leaders. Consequently, he had to leave his religious studies at Mashhad and return to his place of birth, Shahmírzád.* Because of persecution, however, he was unable to reside in that town for very long either. Eventually he settled in Tihrán, where he became a well-known Bahá'í figure to all. He served the Cause of God with distinction and, as a consequence, endured much physical suffering. His name has been immortalized by numerous Tablets he received from Bahá'u'lláh and 'Abdu'l-Bahá and by his biography which is written by 'Abdu'l-Bahá in *Memorials of the Faithful.* Here are a few lines from this book about Ḥájí Ákhúnd:

> This honored man was successful in converting a multitude. For the sake of God he cast all caution aside, as he hastened along the ways of love . . . Again and again he was bound with chains, jailed, and threatened with the sword . . . Things came to such a pass that in the end whenever there was an uproar Mullá 'Alí would put on his turban, wrap himself in his 'abá and sit waiting, for his enemies to rouse and the farrashes† to break in and the guards to carry him off to prison. But observe the power of God! In spite of all this, he was kept safe. "The sign of a knower and lover is this that you will find him dry in the sea." That is how he was . . . Openly at odds with his tyrannical oppressors, no matter how often they threatened him, he defied them. He was never vanquished. Whatever he had to say, he said. He was one of the Hands of the Cause of God, steadfast, unshakable, not to be moved.

---

* A mountain town in the province of Simnan about 150 miles northeast of Tihrán.
† Sergeants-at-arms, footmen.

I loved him very much, for he was delightful to converse with, and as a companion second to none. One night, not long ago, I saw him in the world of dreams. Although his frame had always been massive, in the dream world he appeared larger and more corpulent than ever. It seemed as if he had returned from a journey. I said to him, "Jináb,* you have grown good and stout." "Yes," he answered, "praise be to God! I have been in places where the air was fresh and sweet, and the water crystal pure; the landscapes were beautiful to look upon, the foods delectable. It all agreed with me, of course, so I am stronger than ever now, and I have recovered the zest of my early youth. The breaths of the All-Merciful blew over me and all my time was spent in telling of God. I have been setting forth His proofs, and teaching His Faith." (The meaning of teaching the Faith in the next world is spreading the sweet savors of holiness; that action is the same as teaching.) We spoke together a little more, and then some people arrived and he disappeared.[71]

---

* A title and an honorable way of addressing a person.

# 72

During the ministry of 'Abdu'l-Bahá, the Covenant-breakers,* headed by Mírzá Muḥammad-'Alí, the arch-breaker of the Divine Covenant, and the enemies of the Faith tried their very best to sabotage His work and damage His reputation. With the hope of achieving this goal, they made, in the opening years of the twentieth century, presentations to the government officials and leveled charges against Him. As a consequence of their intrigue and lies, a commission of inquiry was sent to 'Akká by the order of the sultan. Because of all the accusations against 'Abdu'l-Bahá and the false reports that were sent to Constantinople by the Covenant-breakers, the members of this commission had become quite hostile toward 'Abdu'l-Bahá, even before their arrival in the winter of 1907. Their first act was to take over, in effect, the administration of 'Akká. Officials, including the governor, who were regarded as friendly toward 'Abdu'l-Bahá were dismissed. Both the post and the telegraph services were placed under strict scrutiny, and spies were planted around the house of 'Abdu'l-Bahá. Wild rumors were being spread among the inhabitants about the gloomy fate of 'Abdu'l-Bahá. The Bahá'ís were greatly concerned and worried about His safety. But 'Abdu'l-Bahá remained calm and serene through all the commotion, interviews of the commission, supplications of friends, offers of help, and hostile remarks. He continued performing His daily activities that were not curtailed by the unfriendly commission.

Meanwhile, the four members of the commission were receiving twisted information and were busy gathering evidence from the same people who had signed the letter of indictment. The commission remained in 'Akká for a period of one month preparing a dossier against 'Abdu'l-Bahá. In their false report, the Covenant-breakers had accused 'Abdu'l-Bahá of building a fortress for military purposes. So, on a certain Friday, the commission inspected

---

\* Internal opposition to the Center of the Faith is known as "Covenant-breaking," and those who take part in such an opposition are known as "Covenant-breakers."

the mausoleum* that was being built on Mount Carmel. The members of the commission were, apparently, impressed by the strength of the structure and its suitability for a military confrontation with the forces of the government. Shortly after this inspection, they unexpectedly boarded the ship and sailed toward Constantinople.

After this sudden departure, it became known that an attempt had been made against the sultan's life. A few days after this event, the commission submitted its report to the bewildered sultan. But at that crucial time, he and his government were distracted by the more pressing issue of their own survival. Hence, the report against 'Abdu'l-Bahá was essentially ignored, and the hopes of the Covenant-breakers and their cohorts were, once again, dashed into nothingness.

Balyuzi has written, "A few days before the arrival of the Commission of Enquiry 'Abdu'l-Bahá had a dream which He related to the Bahá'ís. He dreamt that a ship sailed into the bay of Haifa, and birds resembling dynamite flew inland from it. The people of 'Akká were terrified, and He stood among them calm and collected, watching these birds. They circled and circled over the town and then went back whence they had come. There was no explosion. 'Abdu'l-Bahá said that danger loomed, but it would pass and no harm would result."[72]

---

* The Shrine of the Báb.

# 73

Shoghi Effendi Rabbáni, better known as Shoghi Effendi, was the Guardian and appointed head of the Bahá'í Faith from 1921 until his death in 1957. He held the explicit authority to interpret the writings of the three central figures of the Bahá'í Faith: the Báb, Bahá'u'lláh, and 'Abdu'l-Bahá. For thirty-six years he worked methodically and vigorously for the establishment of the institutions of the Faith and their development.

Ruḥiyyih Khánum writes:

> Shoghi Effendi was sometimes subject to vivid and significant dreams, both pleasant and unpleasant. It is reported that in his babyhood, he woke one night, crying, and the Master told his nurse to bring Shoghi Effendi to Him so that He could comfort him; the Master said to His sister, the Greatest Holy Leaf, "See, already he has dreams!" . . . . By 1907 he was living with this same nurse, Hájar Khátún, who had always been with him from his infancy, in the newly constructed house of 'Abdu'l-Bahá, which became his last home and later the home of the Guardian. It was here that Shoghi Effendi had a very significant dream which he recounted to me and which I wrote down. He said that when he was nine or ten years old, living with his nurse in this house and attending school in Haifa, he dreamed that he and another child, an Arab schoolmate, were in the room in which 'Abdu'l-Bahá used to receive His guests in the house in 'Akká, where the Master was living and where Shoghi Effendi had been born. The Báb entered the room and then a man with a revolver appeared and shot at the Báb; then he told Shoghi Effendi, "Now it is your turn," and began to chase him around the room to shoot him. At this Shoghi Effendi woke up. He repeated this dream to his nurse, who told him to tell it to Mirza Asadullah* and ask him to tell the Master, Who replied by revealing

for Shoghi Effendi this Tablet. The strange thing, Shoghi Effendi said, is that it was just about this time that 'Abdu'l-Bahá was in great danger and wrote one of His Wills in which He appointed Shoghi Effendi as Guardian.

He is God

Shoghi Mine

This dream is a very good one. Rest assured that to have attained the presence of His Holiness the Exalted One, may my soul be a sacrifice to Him, is a proof of receiving the grace of God and obtaining His most great bounty and supreme favour. The same is true of the rest of the dream. It is my hope that you may manifest the outpourings of the Abhá Beauty and wax day by day in faith and knowledge. At night pray and supplicate and in the day do what is required of you. 'Abdu'l-Bahá[73]

---

* He was a teacher of the Faith from the city of Iṣfahán who rendered many services to the Cause of God, and who eventually became a Covenant-breaker. Bahá'u'lláh had blessed him with the skill of interpreting dreams. See also Dream #76.

# 74

Muḥammad Thabit-i Maraqi'i was a well-known and active Bahá'í teacher. He traveled extensively in Iran and took the message of Bahá'u'lláh to countless people. In one of his teaching trips, he arrived at a very small village a few miles from Maraqeh,* his own birthplace. Rustam, who was a relatively new Bahá'í, lived in this village. His wife, Javahir, had been extremely hostile toward the Bahá'ís. She had been making life very difficult for Rustam who, obedient to the Divine command for kindness and patience, had continued with his life in an attitude of forbearance and resignation. One day he, with much pleading, obtained Javahir's permission to invite Mírzá Muḥammad Thabit-i Maraqi'i and a few of his friends to their home. Thabit-i Maraqi'i has given the following account of what he witnessed in Rustam's house:

> It was a Thursday afternoon when five Bahá'í friends and I arrived at Rustam's house. We were ushered into their humble house where we were first served tea. The house consisted of one room, in middle of which was installed a tanoor.† This one room was accommodating Rustam, his wife, their three children and all their belongings. By looking around you could easily see that this family was a poor one, indeed. The weather had turned cold and the fire was burning in the tanoor. We all sat around this source of heat and began praying, reading the sacred writings and conversing. Javahir and her children were sitting at a corner watching us and listening attentively. After a while they all lay down and went to sleep. We continued with our discussions, reading the Bahá'í writings and reciting some poetry.

---

* An old and historical city in East Adhirbayjan province located in northwestern Iran.
† *Tanoor* or *tandoor* is a sunken clay oven used for cooking in southern, central, and western Asia.

All of a sudden we were startled by hearing the loud and agitated voice of Javahir saying, "O God, I knew not, please pardon my sins. Would you graciously accept my repentance?" Rustam went closer to her, returned and told us that she was perspiring profusely and that she seemed quite distressed. Suddenly, she got up and hurried restlessly toward us. First she kissed the faces of all the friends and then she dropped herself on my feet and began crying and sobbing for about one hour. We all thought that she had really gone mad. Little by little, she regained her composure and began talking.

"Now I know that you are all my brothers. Until tonight I had remained ignorant and had been cursing you and acting extremely rude toward you. For the sake of Him Whom you worship please forgive my offensive behavior. I am repenting now and consider myself, from this moment on, to be one of your sisters and one of the humble hand-maidens of Bahá'u'lláh.

Rustam was quite surprised to hear the name *Bahá'u'lláh* from her lips. He assured us that she had never heard of Bahá'u'lláh before and that, until then, she had known of the name of the Báb only. Then Javahir began to explain:

"Your chanting last night sounded very pleasing to me and strongly attracted my heart. In that blissful condition, I went to sleep and had a dream. In my dream I saw an expansive garden in which were growing many tall and verdant trees. The great door to the garden was made of wrought iron. Through the opening of the door, I could see the inside of the garden and its beautiful flowers of many colors. With some hesitation and fear I entered it and moved forward toward the interior of the garden. Soon, I saw a distinguished siyyid who was wearing a very attractive green turban. He had a beautifully chiseled face and his body was donned with a black 'abá.* I saluted Him with a 'Salaam.'† He smiled at me and returned my greeting with 'Alláh-u-Abhá.' Then He said, 'Javahir, what are you doing here? Do you not know that this garden belongs to me?' I said, 'Sir, may my life be a sacrifice to the Apostle of God, would you please tell me who you might be.' He said 'I am the same Báb whom you curse all the time. I know, however, that you are not aware of the truth, and I have forgiven you. But if it were not for me, the religion of God would have been decimated.' I said, 'Sir, I am very sorry, I would never do that again.'"

"I turned around and wanted to leave the garden when He said, 'Where are you going? Take a stroll and see the garden.' I said, 'Sir, I was afraid You would not agree.' He said, 'No, no, this garden is for the benefit and pleasure of all the people.'

He then went away, and I resumed my walk. Forthwith, I saw a sun shining from one direction of the garden. Soon I realized that the source of that light was not really a sun but a very handsome and dignified man. He was wearing on His head a fez around which was placed a delicate turban. His beard and his shoulder-length hair were white and luxurious. With a majestic and imposing voice He said, 'Javahir, why do you harass and insult my servants?'"

"His voice was so penetrating and imposing that it permeated the marrow of my bones. Every limb of my body began to shake. With a quivering voice I asked Him who He was. He said, 'I am Bahá'u'lláh, the Lord of the

---

* A loose outer garment, resembling a cloak, commonly made of camel's hair.
† The common form of greeting amongst the Muslims, meaning peace.

world.' Instantly, I believed in Him and accepted His pronouncement with all my heart. I prostrated myself before Him, crying and begging for forgiveness. He said, 'If those who were the target of your persecution and enmity do not forgive you, neither would I.' At this point, I woke up in a frightful state of mind."

To be brief, the change in Javahir's attitude affected all of us who listened to her story attentively and burst to crying several times. She was saying that her sins, especially those committed against her husband, were not of the kind to be forgiven. Several times she threw herself at the feet of her husband, crying and begging his forgiveness. Until dawn nobody could sleep. Eventually she became relatively calm under the influence of prayers, sacred writings, and some counseling. By then, we were all exhausted and lay down to rest. Soon, however, we were awakened from our little nap by much commotion and shouts coming from outside the house. I rushed outside and saw that Javahir was attacking a man with a stick because he had said something derogatory against the religion of her husband. I managed to bring that quarrel to an end, and a few days later I left the area.

In subsequent months and years, I kept hearing that Javahir had become a very sincere and active member of that Bahá'í community. She had created much enthusiasm among the Bahá'í women and had been regularly attending the Bahá'í meetings despite the extreme weather conditions prevailing in that mountainous area.[74]

# 75

Dr. Yuness Afroukhteh was 'Abdu'l-Bahá's amanuensis in Haifa from 1900 to 1909. 'Abdu'l-Bahá addressed him as Kh'an. He is the author of the book, *Memories of Nine Years in 'Akká*. He recounts:

> . . . one day in the pilgrim house I had a strange and horrible dream. I saw myself, accompanied by a number of friends, sailing in a small fragile ship. I heard someone say, pointing to a gigantic ship approaching us from some distance away, that the ship was plague-ridden and that the government had ordered it to be destroyed. As the ship approached, the officers of our small ship gave the command to attack. Cannons began to roar, mortar shells exploded and hand grenades were hurled. The large ship was on fire. Flames and a cloud of smoke, as well as the screams, weeping and wailing of those on board, rose heavenward. The shrieking sound of their weeping and sobbing was so heart-rending and harrowing that, as the ship began to sink, I awoke shaken and frightened. In that state of fear and shock, I interpreted that dream as signifying the destruction of the covenant-breakers, and I was confident of the accuracy of my interpretation. Yet, I waited for an opportunity to bring the matter to the attention of 'Abdu'l-Bahá, feeling quite certain that He would confirm my interpretation. The opportunity did not present itself until one day in the presence of a group of resident Bahá'ís and pilgrims, as I gazed in humility and adoration at the sublime countenance of 'Abdu'l-Bahá, He suddenly said. "Kh'an, why don't you say something?" "I have had a dream," I responded. Receiving His permission, I recounted the details, anticipating His affirmation of my interpretation. However, after a moment's pause, He spoke these words with power and authority: "The ship in which you found such comfort is the ship of the Cause of God and the large ship is the ship of the world. This ship is outwardly very small, but the ship of the world will sink, while the ship of the Cause of God will reach the safety of the shore."[75]

# 76

Dr. Yuness Afroukhteh also recounts:

Mírzá Nuru'd-Dín,* who during the recent crisis† was assigned the task of gathering up both the voided and authorized copies of the Holy Writings accumulated over the years in various secret locations, had had a dream one night. When he saw Mírzá Asadu'lláh‡ he asked him to interpret it. He described his dream in these words: "A few nights ago I dreamt that a large jug of attar of rose (which at that time came from Istanbul and cost one gold lira per *mithqal*) broke and the fragrant contents were splashed all over the floor. I was labouring feverishly to recover all I could by picking up handfuls of the liquid and pouring it into a large drum. There seemed to be no end to the expensive fluid, and I was whispering to myself that every few drops that fell from my fingers was worth one gold lira, and so how precious must be the value of this much perfume." Mírzá Asadu'lláh responded, "You will be instructed to gather up the rough drafts and the obsolete copies of the divine verses revealed in recent years and put them in a safe place!" And indeed, that dream was realized that very night. The moral of this story is, first, to demonstrate the gift that was granted to Mírzá Asadu'lláh despite his subsequent heedlessness and infidelity and the unfortunate end that awaited him, and secondly, to show that the government agents were active both covertly and openly, and generally on permanent assignment, which called for constant vigilance. Once or twice things became so critical that the Master gathered together all written materials, and I too collected all my papers and dispatched them to a safe place.[76]

---

* He was 'Abdu'l-Bahá's secretary. His father was Zaynu'l-Muqarrabín, one of the Apostles of Bahá'u'lláh and a well-known scribe.
† This refers to the time when the members of the Inquisition Committee who were hostile to 'Abdu'l-Bahá were still in 'Akká. Refer to Dream #72.
‡ See footnote to Dream #73.

# 77

Juliet Thompson was an early American believer and a talented artist who was greatly devoted to 'Abdu'l-Bahá. As a young girl she went to Paris to further her art studies. There she met May Bolles (Maxwell) who acquainted her with the Bahá'í Faith. Soon she accepted the Faith and began her exemplary services to the Cause for over half a century. The year after the Master's release from the prison city of 'Akká, in 1908, Juliet made her first pilgrimage to Haifa. Next she attained the presence of 'Abdu'l-Bahá in 1911 when He was in Europe. Then on April 11, 1912, 'Abdu'l-Bahá arrived in New York, where Juliet followed the Master everywhere, attending all meetings in New York, Brooklyn, and New Jersey. She eagerly listened to His vivifying words and faithfully recorded in her diary the priceless impressions of those days. These notes, together with her account of many hours in the presence of 'Abdu'l-Bahá, were later published under the title *The Diary of Juliet Thompson*, a true love story. In 1926 she made, with Mary Maxwell, the daughter of her beloved friend and teacher, a second pilgrimage to the Holy Land. After her death in 1956, Shoghi Effendi named her as one of the disciples of 'Abdu'l-Bahá.

The next six dream stories are taken from her diary.

The following discussions and interactions took place during a drive in and around Thonon, Switzerland. With 'Abdu'l-Bahá in the car were Juliet Thompson, Laura Clifford Barney—a renowned Bahá'í who compiled and translated 'Abdu'l-Bahá's *Some Answered Questions*—and Hippolyte Dreyfus-Barney, the first native French believer and Laura's husband. He learned Persian and Arabic in order to translate the writings of Bahá'u'lláh and 'Abdu'l-Bahá.

Then He ('Abdu'l-Bahá) said something to Hippolyte, laughing, and with those vivid gestures of His, continued to talk for some time. What He said I couldn't catch—I know such a tiny bit of Persian—but Hippolyte told me afterward, rather reluctantly! that the Master was speaking about dreams. He had laughed at Hippolyte because he did not believe in them and had explained that there were three kinds of dreams: dreams that come from some bodily disorder, symbolic dreams, and those in which future events are clearly foretold. When the soul is in a state of perfect purity it is able, He said, to receive a direct revelation from God. Otherwise, it sees in symbols.

Then He told us the story of a man, a Christian, who had visited Him in 'Akká and expressed his disbelief in dreams. "But," said the Master, "your own Sacred Writings mention such things." Still the man remained skeptical. A few months later, however, he reappeared in 'Akká, sought the presence of the Master, and immediately fell at His feet and attempted to kiss His hand, which the Master will never allow. "In the Name of Bahá'u'lláh, let me kiss Your hand," pleaded the Christian. He then went on to confess that now he did believe in dreams. He had learned, he said, through a sorrowful experience that the Master had spoken the truth to him. One night when he was away from home he had had an alarming dream of his little daughter. She had come to him, sat on his knee and complained that her head ached. Rapidly she grew worse. They sent for the doctor. The father knew in his dream that she was hopelessly ill and felt the most acute anguish. Then he saw her die. The following night he returned to his home and his daughter came and sat on his knee. "Father," she said, "my head aches." Then followed her illness, her death.

"As the mind has the power when awake to think constructively or to dissipate its powers uselessly, so, when the body is asleep, it can either construct or dream meaningless dreams."[77]

# 78

Juliette recounts:

Once I said to our Lord ('Abdu'l-Bahá): "In a dream one night I saw Thy Face. And it was really Thy Face. I know now. And in my dream I thought: This is a Beauty to follow, leaving everything behind. It is a Beauty to die for."

He leaned forward and looked at me with great solemnity. "That was a true vision," He said, "and you will see it again."[78]

# 79

Juliette recalls:

As I threw back my head to look up at His wondrous Face, my veil slipped off.

"I will fix it for you Myself," He said tenderly. "I will fix it nicely My daughter." And with His electrifying fingers He arranged it all around my face, crossed it at the throat and spread it on my shoulders.

My mind flashed back to a dream—I had it in Paris eight years ago. In this dream I stood in the air with 'Abdu'l-Bahá, opposite Him in the air. His eyes were plunging LOVE through my eyes into my heart, the unimaginable Love of God, a new Revelation to my heart. Then He drew from the breast of His robe a white veil, laying it upon my head, arranging it around my face, crossing it on my shoulders with fingers that charged me with his life—just as He was doing now.

Now, sitting in His room in 'Akká, sitting on the floor at His feet, raising my eyes to that incomparable Face, so beautiful in age, I saw behind its lines the exact structure of the young Face—the never-to-be-forgotten Face of my dream, when I had met Him in the air. "My Lord," I cried. "Once in a dream you put a white veil on my head."

"That I did long ago," He answered.[79]

# 80

Juliette recounts the following story of being on Lake Geneva:

We gathered around Him on the boat (on Lake Geneva), Laura, the Persians, and I, and for a while He sat silent and grave in our midst. Then suddenly He turned and smiled at me.

"You never dreamed, Juliet," He said, "that you would be with Me in a boat."

"I have often dreamed that I was with You in a boat!"

"But you never thought it would be fulfilled in this way!"

"No," I smiled. "I never did. I couldn't have imagined this!"[80]

# 81

Juliette recalls:

I spoke of dear Silvia Gannett: "She asked me to tell You, my Lord, of a dream she had lately in which a voice said to her: 'I want you to serve Me in London.' She felt sure that it was Your voice. But she never mentioned this dream to me till one day she came to see me and found me crying, with Your Tablet in my hand and Aḥmad's letter saying that You would be in London at the Races' Congress. Then, when I explained why I was crying—that Mamma wouldn't let me travel alone—she told me the dream and that now she saw the meaning of it: she must go to London with me. But she could only stay there a very short time, much as she longed to wait till You came. She had to return home to get married."

The Master, at this, smiled so funnily, for Silvia is seventy-two!

Then He said: "It," (her dream, of course, and her obedience) "is a sign that she will make progress and that her work in the Cause will be very good. Tell her it is just as though she had seen Me. Her journey is accepted as a visit. It will be just as though she had seen Me, just the same."[81]

# 82

Juliette records in her diary:

A few nights ago Marjorie* and I had a double dream. In her dream, I was out in space with her. In mine, we were in a room together and the Master had just entered it. He walked straight up to Marjorie, put His two hands on her shoulders and pressed and pressed till she sank to her knees. And while she was sinking, she lifted her face to His and everything in her seemed to be dying except her soul, which looked out through her raised eyes in a sort of agony of recognition.

Today, after one glance at the Master, this was just the way she looked. "Now," she said, "I know!"[82]

---

* Marjorie Morten, a New York Baháʼí and Juliet's close friend.

## 83

'Abdu'l-Bahá's first visit to Paris was in 1911, where He delivered many public talks ". . . in words which were the very breath of the Holy Spirit."* These talks were compiled and published first in 1912 as *Talks Given By 'Abdu'l-Bahá in Paris*, a title which was later changed to *Paris Talks*.

One day, when 'Abdu'l-Bahá was in France, He said to some friends, "Last night I saw the Blessed Beauty in my dream. He was speaking in a language which everyone could understand, but it was different from all other existing languages in the world. I wondered to myself if that was the universal language and if the blessed tablets had been translated into it. Just then we heard another person's voice. Bahá'u'lláh wanted to know who that person was. I went outside and saw a tall and handsome man who had a white beard. He was saying that he had come from the cities of Jabolsa and Jabolqa† . . . Then he said that those two cities were in the heavens. I said to him, 'You must, therefore, be heavenly' and took him to the presence of Bahá'u'lláh. Sheer joy and happiness woke me up."[83]

---

* *Ministry of the Custodians*, p. 87.
† Some <u>Shí</u>'ah Muslims believe that their Twelfth Imám went into concealment over 1100 years ago and has, ever since, been living in these two mysterious cities.

# 84

During His stay in Paris, 'Abdu'l-Bahá received many visitors of diverse backgrounds and persuasions. Just two days before His departure from Paris, He had a visitor from the United States. In *God Passes By*, Shoghi Effendi refers to this visitor from New York in these words: ". . . the extraordinary experience of a woman whose little girl, as the result of a dream she had had, insisted that Jesus Christ was in the world, and who, at the sight of 'Abdu'l-Bahá's picture exposed in the window of a magazine store, had instantly identified it as that of the Jesus Christ of her dream—an act which impelled her mother, after reading that 'Abdu'l-Bahá was in Paris, to take the next boat for Europe and hasten to attain His presence . . ."*

When the visitor was informed that 'Abdu'l-Bahá was about to leave Paris, she related the following:

Oh, how glad I am to be in time! I must tell you the amazing reason of my hurried journey from America. One day, my little girl astonished me by saying: "Mummy, if dear Lord Jesus was in the world now, what would you do?" "Darling baby, I would feel like getting on to the first train and going to Him as fast as I could." "Well, Mummy, He is in the world." I felt a sudden great awe come over me as my tiny one spoke. "What do you mean, my precious? How do you know?" I said. "He told me Himself, so of course He is in the world." Full of wonder, I thought: Is this a sacred message which is being given to me out of the mouth of my babe? And I prayed that it might be made clear to me.

The next day she said, insistently and as though she could not understand: "Mummy, darlin', why isn't you gone to see Lord Jesus? He's told me two times that He is really here, in the world." "Tiny love, Mummy doesn't know where He is, how could she find Him?" "We see, Mummy, we see."

---

* Shoghi Effendi, *God Passes By*, p. 460.

I was naturally perturbed. The same afternoon, being out for a walk with my child, she suddenly stood still and cried out, "There He is! There He is!" She was trembling with excitement and pointing at the windows of a magazine store where there was a picture of 'Abdu'l-Bahá. I bought the paper, found this address, caught a boat that same night, and here I am.[84]

# 85

One day a woman related her dream to 'Abdu'l-Bahá this way: "A young girl became evident to me as belonging with the family, but I could not make out who she was. She spoke of a horse that my son had had long ago, but I did not understand what she meant. After a time it became known that she was my daughter, and I felt grieved to think that I had not been conscious of her presence in all the past years. She seemed not hurt, but surprised that we did not understand her. Just as I was waking, I realized that she was our little baby who had passed away over twenty-one years ago, when nine months old."

After telling her dream, the lady added, "She was my idol, and because I loved her so much, I tried hard to put her out of my thought, and the dream made me feel that we should not do this."

This is how 'Abdu'l-Bahá interpreted this dream: "That child is your trust within the charge of God. She was a child when she went, but you shall find her full grown in the Kingdom of God . . . You shall not find her there as a child. You shall find her perfect and mature. As to the horse once belonging to your son, of which she spoke: Horse in a dream means wish. It shows that your daughter has fulfilled her wish and her desire, and that shows the loftiness of her station. The wish is one in which your son shared, but she attained to it. It is my hope, God willing, he, too, will attain to it."

Surprise was expressed that a child of only nine months could have a wish, and 'Abdu'l-Bahá said: "The child is born with a wish."

The lady was crying, and 'Abdu'l-Bahá continued: "Do not cry. Be happy because you saw her, and you saw her perfected. You must be happy. She is your trust with God. You have not lost her out of your hands. . . . The cause of her surprise is this—that you are crying; your daughter would say: 'I have a good mother. She must be happy. Why does she cry? I am surprised' . . ."

Relative to the comment of the woman that she tried to put the child out of her thoughts, 'Abdu'l-Bahá said: "It is not in man's control when to forget one. It is not good for one to try to forget them. One must always remember them."[85]

# 86

'Abdu'l-Bahá arrived in New York City on 11 April 1912 and set sail back to Europe on 5 December of the same year. During this nine-month sojourn in the United States, He traveled extensively to many parts of the country, and also to Canada, for the sole purpose of proclaiming Bahá'í principles, such as unity of God, unity of the religions, oneness of humanity, equality of men and women, world peace, and economic justice. Writers, poets, politicians, and leaders of thought sought his counsel in private interviews, and seekers of all races and classes attended his public talks. Journalists, struck by his charismatic personality and by the modernity of his teachings, described Him as a "Prophet from the East" and an "Apostle of Peace."

The following is recorded in *Abdu'l-Bahá in New York, The City of the Covenant*: "On the afternoon of June 15, 'Abdu'l-Bahá came down to the waiting crowd of friends. He told them that while resting, He had dreamt that he was speaking to them at the top of His voice. The sound of His own voice awakened Him with the word 'distinction.' He explained the meaning of distinction in every kingdom of Creation. 'I desire distinction for you. The Bahá'ís must be distinguished from others . . . but not of any worldly distinction. For you, I desire spiritual distinction.'"[86]

# 87

On His travels through America, 'Abdu'l-Bahá mainly visited the cities. First, he stayed a week in New York, then He went for a week to Washington D.C., the capital. Next, He went to Chicago for one of the most important events of His journey: the laying of the foundation stone for the building of the first Bahá'í temple in America.

Ten years earlier, the Bahá'ís of Chicago had started with the preparations for this. They had received news of the building of the temple in 'Ishqabad in Russia. From a Persian Bahá'í, they had received a report on the laying of the cornerstone. In his letter, he had encouraged them also to begin building a temple in America. The Chicago Bahá'ís consulted upon this, and before long all its members were at one in support of this proposal. They asked 'Abdu'l-Bahá for His approval of the plan. He was absolutely delighted. . . .

A good deal of money was needed to buy the land for the temple. The American Bahá'ís saved hard for this, sometimes with nickels, dimes, and quarters. They got help from other countries; 'Abdu'l-Bahá encouraged the Bahá'ís in the East to contribute to the building fund. So money came not just from Western Europe but also from Egypt, Persia, India, and South Africa . . .

Some Bahá'ís, such as Nettie Tobin, had very little money but still wanted to give something. Nettie Tobin was a widow, and as a seamstress, she could only just earn enough for herself and her two children. She was sorry she could give so little. She prayed that somehow she would have the chance to give something significant. Then in a dream she heard a voice telling her to look for a stone. She began searching at once and went to a building site near her home. The foreman allowed her to pick out a stone from the pile that the builders were not going to be able to use. She found one and went to a Persian Bahá'í friend to ask for help. Together they went with an old child's pram to the building site, hoisted the stone onto the pram, and went with it to the tram. At first the conductor would not allow them on, but Nettie was able to persuade him to take them. It was not an easy trip because they had to change twice on the way. The other passengers looked at them in amazement. Who were these people getting on the tram with a large stone in an old pram? Nettie took no notice of this. Her goal was fixed; the stone had to go to the site where the temple was to be built. They got off the tram quite near their goal. But they could not go much farther: the pram collapsed. Nettie would not hear of giving up. She spied a boy with a barrow and asked him to help. They got to the temple land and wanted to take the stone right to the middle of the site. But this was not to be. The barrow bumped against something, overturned, and the stone fell on the ground. For two years, it stayed where it fell.

Then the day arrived when 'Abdu'l-Bahá came to lay the first stone. A tent had been put up for the ceremony, with room for about a hundred people, while outside the tent, about another hundred stood. In His address, 'Abdu'l-Bahá predicted that in the future, there would be temples built all over the world. The first temple was the one in 'Ishqabad. The Bahá'ís there had made great sacrifices for the construction of that temple. Around that temple, there would be various other buildings, such as a hospital, a school for orphans, and a home for those with disabilities. He expressed the hope that the same would happen at the temple in Chicago.

After 'Abdu'l-Bahá's speech, the company went outside. 'Abdu'l-Bahá asked them to bring Nettie Tobin's stone, which was still lying somewhere on the site. Meanwhile, He walked up and down and asked where the center of the site was. When the stone was brought, one of the ladies handed Him a leather pouch containing a gold trowel. With this trowel, 'Abdu'l-Bahá tried to dig a hole in the ground at the spot that had been pointed out to Him as the center of the site. It could not be done, as the ground was too hard. So He asked for another tool. A young man ran to a nearby house and fetched a pick-axe. With a powerful stroke, 'Abdu'l-Bahá swung the pickaxe in the air, and with a couple of swings, He was through the sod. In the meantime, another boy had fetched a spade. 'Abdu'l-Bahá took the spade and then asked some of the ladies to begin the digging. Others joined in to dig; there were people of fifteen different nationalities, from Asia, Africa, Europe, and, of course, America. When the hole was big enough, 'Abdu'l-Bahá took a few handfuls of earth and distributed this among some of the bystanders. Then the stone was set in its place. 'Abdu'l-Bahá produced the gold trowel again and, with it, pressed the earth down firmly around the stone . . . Forty years after 'Abdu'l-Bahá had laid the first stone, the temple was officially dedicated.[87]

# 88

On August 20ᵗʰ 1912 a young man arrived at Green Acre* for the sole purpose of seeing 'Abdu'l-Bahá. His name was Fred Mortenson. He was from Minneapolis and had spent many of his earlier days in prison. Albert Hall, a Bahá'í lawyer, had defended him in one of his court appearances and had, subsequently, taught him the Bahá'í Faith. Years later, Mr. Mortenson wrote for the *Star of the West*:

> . . . At this time I was defended by our departed, but illustrious Bahá'í brother, Albert Hall, to whom I owe many thanks and my everlasting good will for helping to free me from the prison of men and of self. It was he who brought me from out the dark prison house; it was he who told me, hour after hour, about the great love of 'Abdu'l-Bahá for all his children and that he was here to help us show that love for our fellow-men . . . Again through the attraction of the Holy Spirit I was urged, so it seemed to me, to go to see 'Abdu'l-Bahá. He was at Green Acre, Maine, at this time, and when I heard the rumor that he might go back to his home (Palestine) and not come west, I immediately determined to go and see him. I wasn't going to miss meeting 'Abdu'l-Bahá after waiting so long to see him.

So, Mr. Mortenson, who was of low financial resources, rode the bumpers on freight trains all the way from Cleveland to Portsmouth, New Hampshire, a place not too far from Green Acre. He has written, "So I left home, going to Cleveland, where I attended a convention of printers for a few days. But

---

* Green Acre, an estate of nearly two hundred acres, lies on the banks of the Piscataqua River in Eliot, Maine. It belonged to Miss Sarah J. Farmer who, after embracing the Bahá'í Faith and visiting 'Abdu'l-Bahá in the Holy Land, offered it to Him. It is now a Bahá'í School, Retreat, and Conference Center.

I became so restless I could not stay for adjournment. How often I have thought about that trip of mine from Cleveland to Green Acre. The night before leaving Cleveland I had a dream that I was 'Abdu'l-Bahá's guest, that I sat at a long table, and many others were there, too, and of how he walked up and down telling stories, emphasizing with his hand. This later was fulfilled and he looked just as I saw him in Cleveland."[88]

# 89

Once a woman came to 'Abdu'l-Bahá and related to Him the following:

Last night, Master, I dreamed that I was in a garden of such beauty that it seemed beyond the power of the most perfect human gardener to have created it. In this garden I saw a beautiful girl, about nineteen, who was caressing the flowers. As I came into the garden she lifted her lovely head and came towards me with outstretched arms, as though in great love and joy at my visit. I look(ed) at her amazed, and then I saw a startling resemblance to the tiny daughter I lost many years before.

[He] smiled His miraculous smile: "My child, you have been permitted to see your daughter as she is now, walking in the sacred garden of one of the worlds of God. This is a bounty of God to you. Rejoice and be happy."[89]

# 90

Mustafay-i-Baghdadi was a devoted Bahá'í who served both Bahá'u'lláh and 'Abdu'l-Bahá with great distinction. He is immortalized by 'Abdu'l-Bahá in *Memorials of the Faithful*: "Muhammad-Mustafa was a blazing light."* His son, Dr. Zia Baghdadi, was a well-known and much-loved figure in the American Bahá'í community for three decades. Like his father, he served 'Abdu'l-Bahá and Shoghi Effendi with much devotion. One day 'Abdu'l-Bahá said to Dr. Baghdadi: "Last night I had a dream. I dreamt that I was in the country and around me were very large boulders. I was near a water spring and on top of me there was a very heavy quilt. I could not move the quilt, as it was very thick and heavy. Then I saw wild beasts coming close to me, such as jackal, bear and fox. They were coming close to me to drink water. I tried to get up but I could not. Then in a loud voice I cried out 'Ya Bahá'ul-Abhá' so that the house shook and the bed cover fell off of me and I woke up and felt comfort."[90]

---

* 'Abdu'l-Bahá, *Memorials of the Faithful*, p. 131.

# 91

In her important and interesting book, Anita Ioas Chapman recounts a story told by her distinguished father, the Hand of the Cause Leroy Ioas. Mr. Ioas related a dream that his Bahá'í friend Albert Windust* had had, many years before. In this dream, Mr. Windust "saw 'Abdu'l-Bahá working very diligently, going to and fro, searching the ground, picking up a twig here, and few pieces of straw there, and finally with these bits and pieces making something with a little shape and form. Albert wrote to the Master asking the meaning of his dream, and 'Abdu'l-Bahá replied: 'I have been commanded to build the Temple of the Lord and I build it with what God gives me!' Leroy concluded his talk, 'Friends, you and I are those twigs, we are those stones, we are those scraps, and the Master is working to shape something out of us. Why should we, unknown and incapable, be quickened by the power of this great spirit and come alive in this day when millions are dying and deprived of spiritual insight? I don't know, and you don't know, but there is only one thing we can do in return for these great gifts and that is to dedicate our lives, purify our deeds, and allow ourselves to become dynamic vehicles which God can use to quicken society."[91]

---

* Albert Windust was a Bahá'í from Chicago and the editor of the *Star of the West* for many years.

# 92

On the ninth of Ridván of the year 1917, Áqa Muḥammad-i-Bolourforoush, a resident of Yazd,* his two Bahá'í friends,† and their families went to a private park for a few days to celebrate the festive occasion. They all returned to Áqa Muḥammad's house on the eve of the twelfth of Ridván. Shortly after their return, he said to his friends, "My friends, I will be killed soon but no harm would come to either one of you two. I say this because last night I dreamed that we were confined in a very inhospitable place of which we all wanted to exit but could not. In my pocket I had a small pen-knife by which I made a tiny hole, about the size of the eye of a needle, in the wall. Then I became extremely thin and managed to go through that small hole. After I got out, I saw the same Malakút (Abhá Kingdom) of which we all have heard. I entered it but cannot describe it to you. The efforts of you two, however, was useless and you could not leave that loathsome enclosure." That night, the three friends spent a few relaxed and happy hours together. Before the two friends left Áqa Muḥammad's house, he told them that they should stop by his shop, some two hours after its opening the following day. From there, they planned to proceed to Mihdí-Abad‡ to join the gathering of the Bahá'ís of Yazd in that village. The next morning, the two friends arrived at the shop [at] the appointed time. They saw that the door to the shop was half open, but Áqa Muḥammad was nowhere to be seen. Later on that day, they were informed that some fanatical people had come to his shop and had taken him to a Muslim religious school, where he had been martyred.[92]

---

\* See footnote to Dream #58.

† Ḥájí Muḥammad-Tahir-i-Malmiri and Áqa Mirza Muḥammad-Thabit Sharqi. Both of them were renowned Bahá'í teachers.

‡ See footnote to Dream #58.

# 93

Ustad Muḥammad Badiei was born in the city of Kashan* to an artisan family of simple means. Following his father's tradition, he began working, as a laborer, in the construction of qanats.† Because of his diligence and innate intelligence, however, he soon became an expert in his profession, and the honorific title of Ustad‡ was added to his name. Due to his expertise in the construction of qanats and his reputation for being able to correctly identify the many problems associated with this system of water delivery, the major farmers and land owners of the area would, at times, require his services.

Among this group of people were a few active and affluent Baháʼís. Some of these Baháʼís were living in Kashan's surrounding villages. Because of the insecurity prevailing over the countryside and the inefficiency§ of the means of transportation at that time, Ustad Muḥammad had to often stay overnight at the homes of his Baháʼí hosts.

Gradually, a few of these Baháʼís became quite impressed by Ustad's personality and by his sense of fairness, and cautiously began introducing him to the Revelation of Baháʼuʼlláh. As time progressed, their discussions became longer and deeper. Since Ustad Muḥammad was under the influence of the great Mujtahid of Kashan, Mullá Habibʼuʼllah, he would report to him his discussions with the Baháʼís. Characteristically, the mujtahid would discourage Ustad from talking with them. Because of his fair-mindedness, however, Ustad would often find himself inwardly agreeing with the expositions of

---

* A city in the central part of Iran about 120 miles south of Tihrán, the capital.

† Qanat is a water delivery system which was developed in ancient Persia and is still used in some arid regions of the world. Qanats tap into the aquifer in a manner that efficiently delivers large quantities of water to the surface without need for pumping.

‡ The title precedes the name and is usually used for well-regarded teachers, artisans, and master-workmen.

§ Ustad Muḥammad's principal mode of transportation was by donkey.

the Bahá'ís. His meeting and discussions with the Bahá'ís of Kashan and its surroundings lasted more than five years.

Then one night, Ustad Muḥammad had a dream. In his dream, he saw himself riding a carriage, but all the roads were closed to him, and he had nowhere to go. Thereupon, he saw an illumined straight path just ahead of him. He awoke from his sleep, and, inspired by this dream, concluded that the lighted path signified the Bahá'í Faith. As a direct consequence of this experience, he joined the Bahá'í Faith when he was in his early thirties. His conversion brought about the awakening of a few members of his family, and today their progenies are present in many parts of the world.[93]

# 94

Lady Sara Louisa Blomfield (1859–1939) was a distinguished early member of the Bahá'í Faith in the British Isles. She was one of the most remarkable women of her age, and she spent the better part of her life in the support and the protection of the rights of women, children, prisoners, and animals. She is now best-known for her involvement in the establishment of the Save the Children Fund and as an active promoter and defender of the Bahá'í Faith. Lady Blomfield was married to the famous architect Sir Arthur Blomfield. She joined the Bahá'í Faith in 1907 and soon became one of its outstanding proponents and historians. She hosted 'Abdu'l-Bahá on His visits to London in 1911 and 1913, followed Him to Paris, and took copious notes of His talks in that city. These notes form the substance of *Paris Talks*, one of the most widely circulated Bahá'í books. As a tribute to her, 'Abdu'l-Bahá bestowed upon her the name Sitárih <u>Kh</u>ánum.* After the passing of 'Abdu'l-Bahá, Lady Blomfield traveled to Haifa, where she interviewed members of Bahá'u'lláh's family. Those recorded recollections, together with her account of the days when she hosted 'Abdu'l-Bahá in London, make up the contents of her book, *The Chosen Highway*. In this book she has written:

When my own mother made the "great change" from one world of God to another, 'Abdu'l-Bahá wrote a very beautiful tablet to me, in which He spoke of my mother as being "in the garden of rejuvenation." One day a friend, who had not yet heard of the tablet of the Master, told me of a vivid dream she had of my mother, whom she had known and loved. "I seemed to be in a marvelous garden, where every type of rare and beautiful flower was in bloom. Moving about among the flowers was a young girl. She seemed to be in a state of inexpressible joy over the loveliness of her garden. Her voice, as she chanted, was full of the ecstasy of a complete happiness. She listened to the song of birds, and

---

* In Persian *Sitarih* means *star*.

inhaled the odor of the flowers as though she were filling her soul with their fragrance. Suddenly she turned towards me, as though conscious that someone was there beside herself. The young girl facing me with an enchanting smile was your mother, in the full beauty of youth."[94]

# 95

Less than eight weeks before His ascension, 'Abdu'l-Bahá had a dream, which He related to His family. This dream is recounted in *God Passes By* by Shoghi Effendi: "I seemed," He said, "to be standing within a great mosque, in the inmost shrine, facing the Qiblih, in the place of the Imám himself. I became aware that a large number of people were flocking into the mosque. More and yet more crowded in, taking their places in rows behind Me, until there was a vast multitude. As I stood I raised loudly the call to prayer. Suddenly the thought came to Me to go forth from the mosque. When I found Myself outside I said within Myself: 'For what reason came I forth, not having led the prayer? But it matters not; now that I have uttered the Call to prayer, the vast multitude will of themselves chant the prayer.'" [95]

# 96

Shortly after the passing of 'Abdu'l-Bahá in November 1921, Lady Blom-field and Shoghi Effendi prepared a compilation on this event. In this doc-ument appears the following, which is 'Abdu'l-Bahá's last recorded dream:

A few weeks after the preceding dream the Master came in from the solitary room in the garden, which he had occupied of late, and said: "I dreamed a dream and behold the Blessed Beauty (Bahá'u'lláh) came and said unto me, 'Destroy this room!' The family, who had been wishing that he would come and sleep in the house, not being happy that he should be alone at night, exclaimed, "Yes Master, we think your dream means that you should leave that room and come into the house." When he heard this from us, he smiled meaningly as though not agreeing with our interpretation. Afterwards we understood that by the "room" was meant the temple of his body.[96]

# 97

After the ascension of 'Abdu'l-Bahá, one of His granddaughters had a dream. She saw in her dream that 'Abdu'l-Bahá was in the same room where He and His sister (the Greatest Holy Leaf) used to pray and have their morning tea. He was talking to her saying, "Why are you so sad and aggrieved? I am happy and satisfied with all of you. For a long time I was longing to see the Blessed Beauty. I was always beseeching Him to admit me into the paradise of His presence. My prayers were answered. I am exceedingly happy and quite comfortable. You should not be mourning and grieving." Then, He advised all to follow the teachings and the instructions of Bahá'u'lláh.[97]

## 98

H. M. Munje, in his book *The Reincarnation Mystery Revealed*, has written:

> Narayenrao Rangnath Shethji (1886–1943),* known as Vakil, was
> the first Bahá'í among the Hindu nation. He had been raised as an
> orthodox Hindu and as a devotee of Lord Krishna, but he came to
> accept that Bahá'u'lláh, who was the return of Lord Krishna, had come
> to the world to bring unity to the religions of mankind. Vakil was
> betrothed to a young girl, Jashodaben (1904–1966), who was a Hindu.
> While on his first pilgrimage to the Holy Land, where Bahá'u'lláh had
> spent the last years of His life as a prisoner and an exile, Vakil asked
> 'Abdu'l-Bahá about his prospective marriage. 'Abdu'l-Bahá replied,
> "Marry the girl to whom you are betrothed and I pray that she may
> become a Bahá'í. . . . In 1929, Vakil went on pilgrimage to the Holy
> Land again, but this time he was accompanied by his wife Jashodaben
> and two lovely daughters. By that time 'Abdu'l-Bahá had passed on
> to the next world and had appointed His grandson Shoghi Effendi as
> the Guardian of the Bahá'í Faith. The Guardian showered love and
> kindness on the whole family.
>
> Jashodaben had always been a great devotee of Lord Krishna and,
> although she loved her husband and was a good wife to him, she did
> not share his beliefs. While in the Holy Land, she spent much time
> with the Greatest Holy Leaf (the daughter of Bahá'u'lláh and sister of
> 'Abdu'l-Bahá) who was the kindest and sweetest person she had ever
> known. There was a woman there who knew Gujarati† and translated
> for her and her children.
>
> Jashodaben continued with her own prayers and worship of Lord
> Krishna until one night when the Guardian sent the family to sleep in

---

* He was born in a well-known Hindu family in Navsari and became a Bahá'í in 1909.
† Gujarati is the language of India's state of Gujarat and some of its adjacent territories.

the Mansion of Bahá'u'lláh in Bahji. Before going to bed, Jashodaben said her prayers as usual and put the Holy Book {Bhagavad Gita} with a picture of Lord Krishna under her pillow. That night Jashodaben had a beautiful dream. She saw a holy Figure in white standing by a cupboard from which he took out beautiful jeweled crowns, one after the other, and gave them to her to put in another cupboard in the room. Every crown was more beautiful than the other, and the holy Figure said to her that these were the crowns of Lord Krishna which now belonged to Bahá'u'lláh. Then she saw Lord Krishna and Bahá'u'lláh together. Lord Krishna took off his crown and gave it to Bahá'u'lláh, and Bahá'u'lláh gave His Taj* to Lord Krishna. Bahá'u'lláh then looked at Jashodaben and said, "There is no difference between us; we are the same."

The next morning Jashodaben woke up very happy and narrated her dream to her husband. Vakil's joy was boundless because he knew that the words of 'Abdu'l-Bahá had now become true and his wife had become a Bahá'í.[98]

---

* See footnote to Dream #47.

# 99

Mrs. Florence Morton was born in Worcester, MA in 1875. One day in 1912 when 'Abdu'l-Bahá was in Boston, Florence was shopping in that city. 'Abdu'l-Bahá walked majestically down the streets of Boston. Crowds going in both directions stared; walked on, each with his own thoughts. Almost a block away, she saw Him and was stirred. He was gone before she could catch up. But Mrs. Florence Morton never forgot the venerable figure seen at a distance. She was later to seek and find 'Abdu'l-Bahá, and to walk in His straight path, serving all the days of her life. Seeking, she found Him; found that she had missed meeting 'Abdu'l-Bahá in person by the length of a city block:

One night in the world of dreams His blessed face appeared to her in a blinding light. "The results of that dream must have been imprinted on my wondering face," she related many years later, "for in the morning my husband looked at me and said, 'What has happened to you?'" From that time (about 1919) nothing could stop her search, nor dim the radiance of her Faith. She studied intensively and served unswervingly, pouring out her material means abundantly and giving of herself, despite opposition of family and friends until she died in 1953.[99]

# 100

The following is a story that has been related originally by Inez, the sister of India Haggarty, who dreamed this beautiful and touching dream. The story came to me (the author) through Mr. Brent Poirier,* who heard it directly from Inez at her home in Carmel, California, around 1980:

Inez's sister, India Haggarty, was a pioneer living in a hotel in Paris in 1931. This was ten years after the passing of the Master, and twenty years after His visit to that city. There was another pioneer in Paris at that time, and I'll call her "Mrs. S." One night in 1931, India had a dream of 'Abdu'l-Bahá. He appeared to her and told her that He wanted her to go, right then, to her Bahá'í sister Mrs. S. "Bring her flowers, and bring her money," He said. India got up out of bed and immediately prepared herself to leave her hotel. As she was fixing her hair in the mirror, her face was still radiant from the vision of the Master. She called down to the hotel clerk to summon a taxi for her and then gathered up all of her money. She set aside the money she needed for her personal expenses and put all the rest of her cash into a small purse. She went downstairs and asked the clerk, "Where is the nearest florist shop?" The clerk answered that there was one quite close by, but as it was just 5 o'clock in the morning, it was of course closed. India said thank you and waited for the taxi. When it arrived, she said to please take her to that florist shop. The driver agreed but repeated what the clerk had said, that the shop was closed. She said, knowing that the Master had a way for her to get flowers, that he should take her there anyway. They arrived, and the windows were all dark. "I told you it was closed," the driver said. India said to take her to the next florist shop,

* He is an attorney in Manchester, NH, USA and a member of the Bahá'í community of that city.

and it, too, was closed. As they drove through the city, they came upon the farmer's market area, where all of the local growers brought in their vegetables and flowers to sell to the local stores. There was a wagon filled with flowers, and India got out of the taxi and went over to the driver. She came back with an armful of red tulips, and got into the taxi. She handed the driver a slip of paper with the address of Mrs. S on it, and they drove across Paris in the early morning darkness.

The taxi dropped India off at Mrs. S's front door, and she stood there, with her arms full of red tulips. She knocked at the door. She heard a rustling, and the door opened. Mrs. S was standing inside, wearing a heavy black coat, and it was obvious that she had been crying. Her face showed great distress. Mrs. S looked at India, and at the red tulips, and cried out, "OH! 'ABDU'L-BAHÁ!" and burst into tears. She sobbed and sobbed. She and India went into her home and sat down, and India tried to comfort her friend. After she was composed, Mrs. S asked India, "Why have you come here?" India answered that the Master had come to her in a vision, and that He had told her to bring flowers, and money. She handed the purse to Mrs. S.

Mrs. S was astounded. When she could speak, she said, "You think I am rich. Everyone does. And I did have money, but I ran out, and I was ashamed to tell anyone. There isn't one speck of food in this house. As you can tell, the house is cold; I cannot afford to heat it. I have been suffering, and I could no longer bear it. I decided last night, to end my life. I awoke this morning, and I went and put on my coat. I decided to cast myself into the Seine, and drown myself. I went to the front door, and was just putting my hand on the doorknob to go out, when suddenly, you knocked. I opened the door, and you were standing there. I could not believe my eyes. Twenty years ago, 'Abdu'l-Bahá came to my house, in this city. And when I opened the door to receive Him, He was standing on my front porch — with an armful of red tulips. And to see you standing there with these tulips, and bringing this money, I could not believe it."[100]

# 101

Mr. Roy Wilhelm (1875–1951) was a prominent American Bahá'í and a wealthy entrepreneur who rendered invaluable services to the Faith, over a period of nearly four decades. In 1908, he met Martha Root and introduced her to the Faith. Mr. Wilhelm was a member of the National Spiritual Assembly of the United States and Canada, often elected as its treasurer. He also acted as a channel of communication between 'Abdu'l-Bahá and the American Bahá'ís. After his death, he was elevated to the rank of a Hand of the Cause of God by the Guardian of the Faith.

On November 12, 1921, 'Abdu'l-Baha sent two messages to Roy Wilhelm. These were the last messages from 'Abdu'l-Bahá received by the American Bahá'ís. The next cable which Roy received from the Holy Land was from the Greatest Holy Leaf, dated 28 November 1921, informing him of 'Abdu'l-Bahá's ascension. ". . . The loss of 'Abdu'l-Bahá was keenly felt by many believers in the fledgling American Bahá'í community. In New York, some Bahá'ís, wishing to create disunity, began to circulate rumours against Roy and Mountford Mills, both members of the Local Spiritual Assembly. Roy, unable to stop the rumours, felt frustrated. However, one night 'Abdu'l-Bahá appeared to Roy in a dream: In the dream, Roy was sitting beside the Master in His high buckboard wagon, with 'Abdu'l-Bahá handling the reins. It was so real that Roy could feel the heat of the Master's body. While driving, 'Abdu'l-Bahá turned, facing Roy squarely, smiling and saying, 'But you would still have Me.' When Roy awoke, that gnawing feeling of having been abused, having been treated unjustly had vanished. . . ."[101]

## 102

Mrs. Jean Stannard was an English lady who was very active in teaching and promoting the Bahá'í Faith. She spent much time in India for the establishment and promotion of the Cause there. She was also the person who established the Bahá'í Bureau in Geneva. 'Abdu'l-Bahá said of her, "Mrs Stannard has dedicated her life to the Cause. She knows neither rest nor comfort. She does not sit tranquilly for one moment."*

In her article, "The Bust of 'Abdu'l-Bahá," Mrs. Stannard tells us the story of *The Bust of 'Abdu'l-Bahá* created by a Russian sculptor, Nicolas Sokolnitsky. The sculptor had become a naturalized French citizen and was living in Paris. In 1936 when Mrs. Stannard was in Paris, some of the Bahá'ís became acquainted with the sculptor and visited him several times at his studio. He always received them with great hospitality. He was in total agreement with the Bahá'í teachings, and believed that the world was rapidly approaching the time when such a spiritual outlook would be generally felt. Mrs. Stannard has related:

> It was on one of these occasions when inspecting some of Sokolnitsky's works as he stood by, that I happened to make the remark, "it is a thousand pities that the great French sculptor Rodin never met the Master when he was in Paris."
>
> Sokolnitsky looked at me suddenly and in tones of great eagerness said, "I will do this! I can do it." His eyes lighted up as he demanded of me what pictures or photographs I had that he could study.
>
> The next day he came to see me and I laid out ready for his inspection all my collection of photos and prints or reproductions that I possessed. He examined these carefully and selected two or three that he thought he could use. . . . It was about noon the next day that I was called to the telephone and his voice in agitated excited tones came through

---

\* 'Abdu'l-Bahá, quoted in *Star of the West*, 5:2:19.

begging me to come to his studio as soon as I could and see what he had done and to tell me something very particular. Thinking he needed some essential information for his work, immediately I put aside some work I was engaged in and left for his studio as soon as I could. To my amazement he uncovered the wet cloth wrapped round a large sized clay bust and I looked on the completed head of 'Abdu'l-Bahá. It was in the rough stage but the likeness to me was unmistakable.

As I stared in astonishment, he laughed and said, ". . . some sculptors would say it was almost miraculous." Then he drew me aside and told me with many touches of descriptive details the following: "The same night that I had the portraits you lent me—it must have been between four and five in the morning—I had a dream so vivid and real of a figure in white standing before me and I saw, I am sure, the Master. He had the turban and white beard and he stretched out a hand to me, and then in Russian said, 'Rise and speak of me.' The effect was so great that on waking directly after, he rose and getting materials together he worked then and there for four or five hours without stopping."[102]

# 103

Amelia Collins, an American Bahá'í, accepted the Faith of Bahá'u'lláh in 1919, and for over four decades gave to it her energetic and single-hearted devotion. The great love she bore for its Guardian, Shoghi Effendi, her loyalty to him, and her desire to render him any assistance she could, in order to lighten the heavy burden that rested on his shoulders, not only endeared her to him but also to all her fellow-believers. For many years, she was a member of the National Spiritual Assembly of the Bahá'ís of the United States and Canada. In January 1951, Amelia Collins was appointed by Shoghi Effendi first to the International Bahá'í Council* and then, in December of the same year, to the rank of Hand of the Cause of God. After the passing of Shoghi Effendi, she was one of the nine Hands of the Cause who remained in Haifa and became known as the Custodians of the Bahá'í Faith.† After serving in this capacity for four years, her weakened and tired body could no longer serve the Faith she loved so dearly. On the first day of January 1962, her blessed soul took flight to the Abhá Kingdom.

At one time Amelia Collins recalled:

> I remember that I was a small child when my father passed away and I was taken to the coffin to have a last look at him. I stood there and peeped into the coffin, and this incident remains vivid in my mind.
>
> During my first pilgrimage, one night I dreamt that I was in the very same position, but that my father arose in his coffin as if awakened.

---

\* International Bahá'í Council (IBC) was an administrative institution of the Bahá'í Faith, first established in 1951 as a precursor of the Universal House of Justice, which came to existence in 1963.

† These nine Hands of the Cause were to exercise all such functions, rights and powers in succession to the Guardian of the Bahá'í Faith, Shoghi Effendi, as were necessary to serve the interests of the Bahá'í World Faith, until the establishment of the Universal House of Justice.

This frightened me so much that I woke up very perplexed. The next day I was to meet the Greatest Holy Leaf, and no one can imagine the condition I was in at the prospect. It was no joke for a humble, insignificant creature like myself to enter the presence of the daughter of the King of Heaven and earth. She, immediately, with her loving and keen insight, understood the great agitation I was in. She very gently asked me how I was; did I sleep well? But not once did I think of my dream. Tea was served, and what a delicious feast, but I was still in the same disturbed state. As I was drinking my tea, she asked me, "Did you have a dream?" She asked me a second time, and suddenly I remembered my dream, and told her about it. She smiled and said, "Of course, your faith in this Cause has brought your father back to life again."[103]

# 104

Tarazu'llah Samandari (1875–1968), the distinguished Hand of the Cause of God, was born in Qazvin, Iran and was brought up in an illustrious family. His father (Samandar) was an Apostle of Bahá'u'lláh and his grandmother was, for a time, in the company of Ṭáhirih. At the age of sixteen, Mr. Samandari had the bounty of being a pilgrim to the presence of Bahá'u'lláh during the last six months of His earthly life. Mr. Samandari's tireless services to the Baha'i Faith spanned the ministries of 'Abdu'l-Bahá and Shoghi Effendi, who in 1951 appointed him Hand of the Cause of God. He was an eloquent speaker and an energetic teacher who traveled extensively throughout the world in the service of the Faith he so cherished.

A very interesting and inspiring biography of Mr. Samandari, in two volumes, was published in 2002. In it are related several of his dreams one of which is the following:

> One day I saw in my Dream a very large tree which had an abundance of leaves and fruits. Upon the branches of this tree were sitting only women, and the men were on the ground looking at that strange scene. Shortly after that dream, the Guardian sent a cable to the Bahá'ís in Iran allowing the membership of the women in that country's national and local spiritual assemblies.
>
> Until then, the Iranian women were temporarily excused from membership in these important Baha'i administrative institutions. This was because of the prevailing conditions in Iran and the social and educational disadvantages that the women were facing at that time.[104]

# 105

Agnes Alexander was an American Bahá'í who was born in Hawaii in 1875 and became a Bahá'í in 1900. At the suggestion of 'Abdu'l-Bahá, she moved in 1914 to Japan, where she lived the rest of her life. She was very active and effective in proclaiming and teaching the Bahá'í Faith in that country. Encouraged by 'Abdu'l-Bahá, she studied Esperanto and became a member of the Universal Esperanto Association. She used her ties to Esperanto to break down language barriers and to talk to others about the Bahá'í Faith. In 1957, she was appointed a Hand of the Cause of God by Shoghi Effendi. She passed away in Hawaii in 1971.

The following story is taken from her writings:

Mr. Tokujire Torii was probably the first blind Japanese who became a Bahá'í. He was an Esperantist at the time and his first supplication to 'Abdu'l-Bahá was written in Esperanto. In his home library, Mr. Torii had many Braille volumes of the writings of Bahá'u'lláh and 'Abdu'l-Bahá transcribed from the English editions. From these volumes he managed to create a Braille book in Japanese for the blind people of Japan. The book was entitled *A Message of Light*. He sent one copy of this book to a Japanese woman who had lost her sight and hearing.

*A Message of Light* became the means of her awakening. Reading with her finger tips its pages, she came into the joy of the knowledge of the Bahá'í Revelation and in a dream had the blessing of a visit from 'Abdu'l-Bahá. Of this experience she wrote to me, "Even though one has eyes and ears he cannot see 'Abdu'l-Bahá because He is far away, but I could meet Him. With sightless eyes and deaf ears I saw and heard Him in a dream and this is the utmost happiness in the world. This bounty came from God and I thank 'Abdu'l-Bahá heartedly."[105]

# 106

Agnes Alexander also recounts:

On January 4, 1937, I received a letter from Louise Bosch* in which she related two dreams she had had. She thought that they concerned our dear Yuri San.† In my diary that day I wrote: "Louise Bosch's letter gives new inspiration that with unity and Divine help the flower of Yuri San (Yuri means lily) will blossom." In one of the dreams Louise saw a great heap of all kinds of rubbish piled high up. The place seemed to be in Japan.

Through a small opening in the pile, to her great astonishment she saw a baby lying in the midst of the rubbish. It looked well and smiling, although the only light it received was through the opening. When I reached Haifa I told the Guardian of the dream. He said briefly that it symbolized the struggling Faith of Bahá'u'lláh in Japan.[106]

---

* Louise Bosch and her husband John Bosch were two outstanding Bahá'ís who donated their property at Geyserville, California, for the purpose of establishing a Bahá'í school.

† Miss Yuri Mochizuki was the first Japanese woman to become a Bahá'í.

# 107

Ali-Akbar Furutan (1905–2003) was a learned and very active Bahá'í in Iran who was appointed a Hand of the Cause of God by Shoghi Effendi in 1951. Prior to this appointment, he had served the Faith as the headmaster of a Bahá'í school, a member of the Local Spiritual Assembly of Tihrán and a member of the National Spiritual Assembly of Iran. For many years he served in these two administrative bodies as their secretary. From 1957 to 1963, he served as one of the nine Custodians at the Bahá'í World Center in Haifa. In his book *The Story of my Heart*, he has related the following account:

When my father became a Bahá'í, his mother and his wife who were both fanatical Shí'ah Muslims vehemently opposed him. His mother was so disturbed by her son's conversion that she went to the mujtahid of the town to seek the death sentence of her only son. The mujtahid was, however, a good-natured man and refused to issue the death sentence on the grounds that my father might be mentally unbalanced. But the miserable family situation continued for many years until one night my mother had a dream. In her dream "an Imám with a radiant countenance and piercing eyes appeared to her. My mother hastily ran to him to pay her respects but the Imám declared that she should leave him as 'thou are not one of our faithful Shí'ahs.' My mother then clung to his garment and tearfully said 'May my life be a sacrifice to thee, I have not neglected my religious duties. I have continually attended the commemoration of the martyrs of Karbilá. I have always been present at those gatherings, mourning the martyrdom of the Prince of Martyrs (Imám Husayn). My children and I are always busy visiting the shrines of the Holy Ones. I have continually given offerings. What wrong have my hands wrought that thou dost not permit me to be in thy presence?' The Imám replied, 'All thou hast mentioned is true; however, for what reason hast thou afflicted thy husband who has believed in the Promised One (Qa'im), who treadeth the Straight Path? And why hast thou tormented him with a new torment every moment?' My mother then wept in her sleep and the Imám disappeared. The cries of my mother awoke my grandmother, and in response to her question as to the cause of this weeping and wailing, my mother recounted her dream. It was the hour of dawn and they both went to my father's room and related to him what had passed. From her description my father understood that the Imám in my mother's dream was no One but 'Abdu'l-Bahá and asked my mother whether she could recognize the Imám if she saw His picture. He then unveiled to her the portrait of the Master which lay hidden with the Bahá'í books in a safe cupboard. My mother confirmed whole-heartedly that the Imám was indeed the same person. My father then, for the hundredth time, began to recount the Master's life and the beliefs of the people of Bahá. Fortunately, at the hour of dawn, they finally awoke from their slumber and the light of faith illumined their hearts and souls." [107]

# 108

Mr. Furutan has also related:

I was the secretary of both [the] National Spiritual Assembly of Iran and the Local Spiritual Assembly of Tehran, and my responsibilities, in view of my poor health, were a little overwhelming. One day as I was preparing to go to my office, I felt a serious weakness in my body. A physician was called who diagnosed measles, but as I showed no signs of recovery at home, I was transferred to the hospital. Fifty days passed and fever still persisted, for at that time there were no antibiotics available and treatment of such diseases usually took a long time. One night, however, I had a dream of the beloved Guardian. He had a flower in his hand and had come to visit me. I tried to stand up in respect, but weakness overtook me and I failed in my effort. He said, "I have brought you this flower." I took the flower, inhaled its fragrance, kissed it, poured some water from a crystal jug beside my bed into a glass, and put that flower, which had three buds, in the glass. Then the beloved Guardian disappeared. I remember having told myself in my dream that attaining the presence of the Guardian meant health and recovery, and three buds indicated that after three days my fever would break. On the following evening, the nurse came and took my temperature and gave me the good news that the fever had finally broken after fifty days! I should mention that a few days before the dream I was given a message from the beloved Guardian in which he assured me of his fervent prayers and asked me to cable news of my recovery. Three days after the dream I was able once again to sit on my bed and began eating simple foods. I gradually regained my health and was discharged.[108]

# 109

Amatu'l-Bahá, Rúhíyyih Khánum (1910–2000), was the wife of Shoghi Effendi who was the head (Guardian) of the Bahá'í Faith from 1921 to 1957. She was born in New York City and her original name was Mary Sutherland Maxwell. After her wedding to Shoghi Effendi in 1937, she became known to the Bahá'í world as Amatu'l-Bahá Rúhíyyih Khánum.* She and her husband became constant companions, and later Shoghi Effendi referred to her as his "shield" and his "helpmate."† Rúhíyyih Khánum served as her husband's principal secretary for many years. In 1951, Shoghi Effendi appointed her to the International Bahá'í Council and in 1952 as one of the Hands of the Cause of God. After the passing of her husband, she served as one of the nine Custodians at the Bahá'í World Center in Haifa from 1957 to 1963. Between July 1969 and April 1973, she traveled extensively throughout Africa visiting the Bahá'ís and taking the message of Bahá'u'lláh to the countless towns and villages in that continent.

In one of her meetings with the Bahá'ís of Ethiopia, she stressed the importance for the Bahá'ís not to dissipate their spiritual energies in being either "for" or "against" current social issues and recounted a dream she had heard from one of the early American believers many, many years ago. It had happened during the lifetime of 'Abdu'l-Bahá, when she herself was a young girl. The lady who recounted it said she had seen a terrible flood of mud engulfing the world, and had witnessed the people in their agony trying to pull each other out of the mud. Sometimes they would succeed in pulling one person out and at other times they were pulled into the mud themselves and drowned. The dreamer had then gone in search of 'Abdu'l-Bahá and found Him on the summit of a hill, busy with some machinery. With anguish of heart she called to Him, "'Abdu'l-Bahá, 'Abdu'l-Bahá!" At first He did not

---

* *Amatu'l-Bahá* means *Handmaiden of Glory.*
† Shoghi Effendi, *Messages to Canada*, p. 22.

pay any attention, until she pulled His sleeve and called His name again and again. Then He asked her what she wanted, and she said, "'Abdu'l-Bahá, the people of the world are engulfed in a sea of mud, they are all drowning, come and help them!" 'Abdu'l-Bahá said, "Don't you see? I am busy making this machinery to absorb and dry up the mud." Rúhíyyih <u>Kh</u>ánum told her audience that this dream was really a graphic picture of the World Order of Bahá'u'lláh. To participate in one struggle against a single form of injustice or a strike against another was not going to solve the global, political, and spiritual problems of mankind.[109]

# 110

In her meeting at a village in the Democratic Republic of Congo, Rúhíyyih Khánum told the friends "of the power of reciting "Ya Bahá'u'l-Abhá" or "Alláh-u-Abhá." Then she told them of her own experiences and dreams and recalled a dream she had had in her youth. She had dreamt that she was in a small canoe on a gigantic river; the canoe had capsized, and she had hung onto a piece of driftwood, drowning, and this had caused her such fear that her heart was frozen. And then she had started reciting "Alláh-u-Abhá" over and over again, and calm and assurance had filled her heart until she found herself on the other shore. Another time, again in her youth, she dreamt she was in an open car, traveling, when suddenly a most frightful creature of the wild attacked her. This creature had half the body of a man and half of an animal and looked ferocious. She was terrified and had started reciting "Alláh-u-Abhá" repeatedly, when all of a sudden she noticed that the creature had changed into a harmless and beautiful being. She then explained that to recite these precious words would remove the fear of witchcraft and witch doctors.[110]

# 111

In the village of Mmutlane,* Rúhíyyih Khánum talked to a small gathering of people about dreams and true prophetic dreams. In particular, she talked about dreams ". . . such as that of the father of Bahá'u'lláh when He was still a young child. She told them that he dreamed that this remarkable Son was swimming and many fish were around Him, each holding to a hair of His head. The interpretation of the soothsayers was that when He grew up He would be followed by multitudes who would hold on to His Words. Then she told of a dream of Shoghi Effendi's which confirmed his decision in choosing Rúhíyyih Khánum to be his wife. He had dreamt that he was in a large ship going to North America and the Captain of the ship was 'Abdu'l-Bahá. They reached the shores of America and then took a train, and the train eventually stopped at a station; when he looked at the sign in the station, it showed the word "Montreal."†[111]

---

* A village in the Central District of Botswana.
† Rúhíyyih Khánum lived in Montreal at that time.

# 112

In *The Priceless Pearl*, Rúhíyyih Khánum has related:

The Guardian was truly an extraordinary man. There is no end to
the examples that come to mind when one thinks of his nature and
his achievements. He had a heart so faithful to those who were faithful
to him that its counterpart could scarcely be found. In the gardens,
on the terrace in front of the Shrine of the Báb, there stands a small
cement room, little larger than a big box. This was the room of Abu'l
Kasim, a keeper of the Shrine dearly loved by Shoghi Effendi for his
devotion and his character. The night before this man died, Shoghi
Effendi told me he had had a strange, twice-repeated dream in which
the green covering of verdure on the Shrine had withered away as if
it had been burnt off. He was much puzzled by this, for he felt it had
a significance. When news was brought to him some hours later that
the keeper of the Shrine was dead he at once understood the dream's
meaning. At different times, over a period of many years, when the
Guardian was building the Shrine and extending the terrace in front of
it, he destroyed this room, but each time rebuilt it, a little farther to the
west, because of the association it had with this devoted soul.[112]

# 113

Dorothy Baker was a prominent American believer who was an active teacher and a great speaker. For many years she served as a member of the National Spiritual Assembly of the Bahá'ís of the United States. On December 1951, she was appointed a Hand of the Cause of God by the Guardian. In January, 1954, on her way back to the United States from an extensive teaching tour, she was killed in an airplane crash over the Mediterranean Sea. Dorothy Gilstrap, in her book *From Copper to Gold*, writes:

Gloria Faizi, wife of the Hand of the Cause 'Abu'l-Qasim-Faizi and a Bahá'í writer, thoughtful, active teacher in her own right, was then pioneering in Arabia with her family . . . Shortly after the accident she called on an Arabian friend whose daughter had been killed in the same Comet [passenger plane] on her way back to school in England. When Mrs. Faizi arrived the woman was surrounded by weeping friends. As there seemed no hope of speaking with her, Mrs. Faizi simply gave the lady a copy of *The Open Door*, a pamphlet dealing with life and death from the Bahá'í perspective, and briefly spoke a few words of sympathy. Several days later the woman contacted Gloria Faizi. She said the booklet had been her only source of comfort and asked Mrs. Faizi to pay her another visit. The two ladies talked for some time about the Bahá'í Faith, then Mrs. Faizi told the grieving mother that the Bahá'ís had also lost someone precious on the same flight and showed her a photograph of Dorothy Baker. On seeing the picture the woman* took it in her hands. She said, "But I know her . . . this is the lady who comes to my dreams night after night and tells me, 'Don't grieve for your daughter. She is very happy. She is with me and I am caring for her.'"[113]

---

* According to the Hand of the Cause of God Dhikru'lláh Khadem (in the *Vision of Shoghi Effendi*, p. 111), this lady accepted the Bahá'í Faith after her dream.

# 114

Mr. William Sears was an American Bahá'í. He authored eleven books and became a well-known international Bahá'í teacher. In 1957, he was appointed as a Hand of the Cause of God by Shoghi Effendi, the Guardian of the Bahá'í Faith. Mr. Sears was born in 1911 in Minnesota and passed away in 1992 in Arizona.

William Sears was only eighteen months old when he accompanied his father to the railroad station at Aitkin, Minnesota one day to receive his aunt. The father and the son were standing on the platform and scanning the train, unsure from which car his aunt would emerge, and "the young lad's focus suddenly locked on a man looking out from one of the exits. Ethereal in appearance, the stranger was a vision in white: flowing ankle-length robe, turban, and long, snowy beard to match.* Never had the youngster seen anyone like him—not even in picture books." The night of that same day, he had his first dream of this stranger, a vision in white. Other dreams about Him followed well into Mr. Sears's adulthood: "They were happy dreams— full of promise—with the man in white beckoning him in one dream to 'fish like Peter.'"

Mr. Sears met and married Marguerite Reimer. In *Lights of Fortitude*, by Barron Harper, we read, "Meanwhile, 'Abdu'l-Bahá wouldn't leave Bill alone. On returning home from his honeymoon Bill dreamed again of the shiny man. In the dream he was seated on a rock while the familiar figure came rushing by on a pair of skis, His white beard flowing in the breeze. Beckoning William to follow, they raced together down the hill, the winter rapidly retreating into spring-like warmth as they descended. Below, William could see a valley with a city nestled within. The shiny man pointed down and said to his companion, 'This is the city' then he vanished and Bill woke up."†

---

* Many people have described 'Abdu'l-Bahá's physical features in these terms.
† Harper, *Lights of Fortitude*, p. 498.

Mrs. Sears has written that while they were living in Salt Lake City, they would take occasional drives to explore the area. She continued:

During one trip into the mountains, I was at the wheel when Bill suddenly said, "Stop. Go down that lane." There was such a strange look on his face. I complied and we arrived at an area overlooking the city. I was moved by the physical beauty of the view before me, but Bill was more deeply stirred. He then shared with me a dream he had had soon after we married. We were then standing in the very place that he had been standing in his dream. The central figure in the dream was the same "Man in White" he so often dreamt of during his life. In this particular instance, the man had come on skis, beckoning Bill to join him. He produced a pair of skis for Bill, and together they skied down the slope and ended where we had now parked our car.

I believed I knew who his "Man in White" was and I showed him a photograph of 'Abdu'l-Bahá. Bill instantly recognized Him as the man he had first seen on the train so many years ago, and so often since in his dreams.[114]

# 115

Dhikru'lláh Khadem was a well-known Bahá'í who was born into a distinguished family in Tihrán, Iran. At the young age of thirty-four, he was elected to the National Spiritual Assembly of Iran and served on that body for twenty-one years. In 1952, Shoghi Effendi appointed him as a Hand of the Cause of God. Mr. Khadem spent the rest of his life in teaching, traveling, and encouraging the Bahá'ís all over the world. He attended many conferences, conventions, and Bahá'í schools and gatherings, first on behalf of Shoghi Effendi and later for the Universal House of Justice. His services continued until his soul took its flight to the Abhá Kingdom in November 1986.

Shoghi Effendi passed away in November 1957. Just before leaving this world, he gave Mr. Khadem an international assignment. In his cable, Shoghi Effendi directed Mr. Khadem to visit the friends in the Scandinavian and Benelux* countries. After the passing of Shoghi Effendi, Mr. Khadem wrote, "When I was on this assignment in the Benelux countries, I was so weary; I looked miserable. The friends could not comfort me. The reason was that while in Brussels, I had dreamed that the Greatest Holy Name fell down to the floor, and a great, great funeral took place. I could not understand it. I thought that perhaps Hand of the Cause Mr. Samandari, loved by everybody, was going to pass away. I was unable to sleep at night because I was crying. The people in neighboring hotel rooms complained to the manager asking him to change my room. I cried; I could not sleep. In the end, we found out what the significance of the dream was: the passing of the beloved of all hearts, Shoghi Effendi. The great, great funeral in my dream happened in reality."[115]

---

* Benelux is a union of three neighboring countries in Europe: Belgium, the Netherlands, and Luxembourg.

# 116

Enoch Olinga joined the Bahá'í Faith in his home country, Uganda, in 1952 and became the most prominent African believer. Due to his efforts and successes in teaching the Cause of God in that continent, Shoghi Effendi gave him the title of Abu'l-Futuh (Father of Victories). He was also given the title of Knight of Bahá'u'lláh* because he was the first Bahá'í who pioneered to British Cameroon. In October 1957, at the age of thirty-one, he was appointed by Shoghi Effendi as a Hand of the Cause of God.

Mr. Olinga became a Bahá'í in February 1952. In August of 1958, he embarked on his journey to his pioneering post, British Cameroon.† With him were Mr. and Mrs. Nakhjavani‡ and two other new Bahá'ís who were also going to their pioneering posts. These two pioneers were first dropped at their respective destinations, after which the Nakhjavanis and Olinga drove on. The journey through the deep tropical jungles of Gabon was long and very difficult. The road was awful, and the area was plagued by insects and diseases. Their vehicle was constantly getting stuck in the mud. The road was so bad that in one day they could travel only fifteen miles. At one point, Olinga separated from the Nakhjavanis and walked thirty-five miles in search of help. When the Nakhjavanis found him the following day, he was exhausted from bad dysentery, in pain, and very worried over the safety of the Nakhjavanis. On reaching the next town, Mr. Olinga was so ill he was hospitalized for two days and could not travel for a week. He told the Nakh-

---

* The title given by Shoghi Effendi to the Bahá'ís who opened new territories to the Faith during the Ten Year Crusade, the Guardian's worldwide expansion plan that began in 1953 and ended in 1963.

† Formerly, it was a British Mandate territory in West Africa. Today, the territory forms parts of Nigeria and Cameroon.

‡ Mr. Ali Nakhjavani and his wife Violette pioneered from Iran to Africa in 1951. Mr. Olinga was one of the many who accepted the Bahá'í Faith through their selfless services and teaching efforts. Mr. Nakhjavani was a member of the Universal House of Justice from 1963 to 2003.

javanis that "the night before, when he was alone with only strange Africans around him with whom he could not talk, afraid for his safety and the money he was carrying, full of misgivings and doubt, asking himself why he had left home and family on such a mad undertaking, he dreamed of Shoghi Effendi, who took him in his arms and held him close, and into him had poured comfort and reassurance; this dream restored his strength and affected him so profoundly he cried out in his heart to the Guardian that he was willing to go through such hardships for him every day of his life!"[116]

# 117

Dr. Rahmatullah Muhajir was a fourth generation Bahá'í from Iran. After marrying Iran Furutan in 1954, he and his wife pioneered to the Mentawai Islands of Indonesia. This was during the Ten-Year Crusade. For this pioneering service, Dr. and Mrs. Muhajir were both named Knights of Bahá'u'lláh by Shoghi Effendi. In October 1957, he was appointed a Hand of the Cause of God by the Guardian, who passed away in November of the same year. The Muhajir family left Indonesia in 1958. For the next twenty-one years, he was constantly on the move, traveling all over the world and inspiring the Bahá'ís to pioneer and to participate in mass teaching campaigns. In 1979, while he was visiting Ecuador, he had a heart attack that ended his earthly life.

After Dr. Muhajir's death, his wife, Iran Furutan Muhajir, wrote his biography and published it under the title *Dr. Muhajir, Hand of the Cause.* In this book, she states, "He very often had dreams which showed him his course of action, and he prayed at length for guidance in his travels." She relates the details of several of his illuminating and guiding dreams. Below is one of his dreams.

While Dr. Muhajir was traveling to different countries and encouraging the friends, Mrs. Muhajir was serving as a Counselor in Southeast Asia. At one time, Dr. Muhajir was suggesting to her that Korea might be a better place for her to settle. One day, Mrs. Muhajir writes, "he told me that he'd had a dream of 'Abdu'l-Bahá. The Master had been standing in front of a world atlas and pointed with His finger to Korea with a strong emphatic gesture. Dr Muhajir told me, 'You should go to the place where you are needed most.' In May 1978 we settled in Korea."[117]

# 118

In her book, Mrs. Muhajir also relates another of Mr. Olinga's significant dreams: "Rahmat told me that Olinga had once had a strange dream that he and Rahmat were standing together, looking down on the earth beneath them. Flames were rising out of every corner, and they could hear screams. Olinga turned to Rahmat and said it was good that they were not in the carnage, and that they were the ones who had been spared. Rahmat believed this meant that he [Rahmat] would soon join his departed friend in the Abhá Kingdom, and leave behind the toils and troubles of this world. Little did I suspect that this intimation would prove correct so soon."*[118]

---

* Mr. Olinga was murdered in September, 1979, and Dr. Muhajir died in December of the same year.

# 119

Mr. Adib Taherzadeh belonged to a prominent Bahá'í family of Yazd, Iran. To pursue his studies in higher education, he moved to the United Kingdom in 1948. He actively served the Faith in that country for forty years, and was elected and/or selected to the membership of local, national, and regional administrative bodies in Great Britain and Ireland. He continued with his services in the continent of Europe until 1988, the year in which he was elected to the membership of the Universal House of Justice. He passed away in January 2000, in Haifa, Israel, the Bahá'í world headquarters. He was a gifted and accomplished writer who wrote several books on the history and teachings of the Bahá'í Faith.

Ian Semple, the subject of Mr. Taherzadeh's dream, was also a member of the Universal of Justice from 1963 to 2005. Mr. David Hofman, the other person mentioned in the following account, was another member of the same body from 1963 to 1988.

At a weekend school in Dublin, in 1961, Adib Taherzadeh was talking about the effect of our good deeds on our descendants and he related the following story:

Some years ago he had attended a Bahá'í public meeting in Oxford where David Hofman was the speaker. He noticed that the only non-Bahá'í who had attended the meeting was a young man who was a student at the university. He seemed very interested in the subject and asked many questions that were answered to his satisfaction by David.

That night Adib had a dream in which he saw the same young student, sitting at a desk covered with papers, and he was throwing these papers away into a wastepaper basket. Adib asked the young student what he was doing. And he replied that these papers were left to him by his ancestors and he was getting rid of them. Then suddenly he stopped, held a large sheet of paper in his hands and stared for a few moments, then turned to Adib with a smile and said "Look! What my ancestors have left me"! When Adib looked he saw a beautiful inscription of the Greatest Name in gold.

When he woke up he knew the young student would become an outstanding Bahá'í. This young student was Ian Semple![119]

# 120

Mr. Masimian was a Bahá'í of Armenian background. Soon after becoming a Bahá'í, he was employed at the American Embassy in Tihrán as a driver. One day, he related to a friend a chance meeting which he had with another Bahá'í who was unknown to him:

On holidays, a group of high-ranking Embassy employees would usually go hunting and return to town by the evening. Naturally, I would drive them wherever they wanted to go. Since I was very much interested in and attracted by the Bahá'í writings I would always carry a Bahá'í book in the car, so that I could read it whenever I got a chance. One Friday, as usual, we drove toward the Chaloos road.* There were many workers and laborers all along the road because there was, in those days, much road-building activity in progress. We asked these people if they knew of any good hunting locations. One of the workers who knew the area well told us that we should park where we were talking to him and climb to the higher grounds where there would be plenty of game animals. I, therefore, parked the car at the side of the road while the hunters, taking their guns and backpacks, got ready to climb. At this point my eyes spotted a poor man, with worn out clothing, who was sitting on a heap of dirt upon the hillside. At the sighting of our car, he stood up and began staring at us. The hunters asked me to accompany them, but I was really more interested in reading my Bahá'í book. I, therefore, told them that I was somehow suspicious of that man on the hill, and that I did not think that it would be safe to leave the car unattended there. So, I offered this as an excuse.

---

* Chaloos Road is an important road for the people of Tihrán, the capital of Iran. It connects this city to Chaloos near the Caspian Sea and some other tourist attractions in northern Iran.

After the departure of the hunters, I began reading my book and, at the same time, watching the poor man out of the corner of my eye. When he saw that my friends were quite far from the car, he climbed down the hill and, to my surprise, moved toward the car. I was sitting in the driver's seat and, because of the prevailing heat, had rolled down the windows. First, I pretended not to have noticed him and continued reading the book. But I could not really concentrate and was cautiously watching the man. Soon, he was standing right next to the window of the car. I looked at him angrily and with a sullen face so that he would go his own way. Without paying any attention to my obvious irritation, he calmly said, "Sir, what is this book that you are reading?" At this point, I lost all my patience and, with a threatening and provocative voice, I said, "It is none of your business what book I am reading. Suppose I tell you the name of the book, what would that mean to you? The Book which I am reading is the Book of Iqán." Before I could finish my words, the man said loudly, "Alláh-u-Abhá, you must be a Bahá'í." Then, he continued, "I am a laborer working on roads. It has been four months now since I left my village and my family behind. I have been dying to see a single Bahá'í and to hear the chanting of a Bahá'í prayer. Last night, with this longing in my heart, I went to sleep. Then, I had a dream in which 'Abdu'l-Bahá appeared. He said to me, 'Tomorrow go to the top of that hill, we will come to visit you.' Today is Friday and I am not working. At the crack of the dawn I came to this hill and have been, ever since, sitting there and waiting. When I saw your car, I became hopeful and came forward to check if my dream would come true."

After hearing his story, I burst out of the car and hugged him very tightly. We kissed each other and cried much and shed, copiously, tears of happiness and exaltation. Then we sat down together and I shared with him the recent Bahá'í news of that time. We ate lunch and had tea together, chanted some prayers and held a small Feast there. We were quite absorbed in our visiting and discussions and didn't realize the quick passage of time. At the sunset my companions returned and were surprised to see the two of us in that condition. They asked, "Is not this man the one whom you did not trust? How is it that you are now like two brothers sitting together and sharing your food?"[120]

# 121

Mona Maḥmúdnizhad was a young high school girl in Iran. She was arrested in October 1982 by the government officials of the city of Shíráz. She, together with nine other Bahá'í women and girls, was hanged in June 1983. Their only crime was membership in the Bahá'í Faith. In order to make their captives recant their Faith, the judges and their revolutionary guards subjected them to much pressure, abuse, and torture during the term of their imprisonment. The officials made one last attempt to break the will of the prisoners and cause them to renounce their Faith. Demonstrating their inhumanity, the authorities began hanging the women one by one while the others were forced to watch the process. But each one of them stood firm and steadfast, as a mighty and majestic mountain, to her last breath. At the time of her execution, the courageous Mona walked resolutely to the rope, kissed the noose and put it over her own head, beating the executioner to his assigned task. Before her martyrdom, Mona had two dreams and some prophetic words that she told her mother, according to the following account:

Ten months before she was killed, Mona had an extraordinary dream which was later related by family and friends. Following is the version transcribed from her diary. She had been saying prayers with a small group of friends for several hours. After they left her home, she was so moved by the prayers that she went into the living room and sat down in front of a photograph of 'Abdu'l-Bahá, meditated quietly and then fell asleep. In her dream, she saw 'Abdu'l-Bahá's chair and desk, with a vase on it, as in the picture before her. She was very happy and said: "How happy I am to see your desk and chair." At the same moment she saw Bahá'u'lláh entering the room. The Blessed Beauty went out into an adjoining chamber and brought out a box containing a beautiful red cape. He unwrapped it in front of her, saying, "This is the cape of martyrdom in my path. Do you accept it?" Mona was speechless with happiness. Finally, she said, "Whatever pleases you . . ." Bahá'u'lláh put the cape back in the box and returned to the adjoining room bringing back with him a second box, containing a black cape which he unwrapped and said: "This black cape symbolizes sorrow in my path. Do you accept it?" Mona replied, "How beautiful are the tears shed in thy path." He put the cape back in the box and again returned to the other room, emerging with yet a third box containing an elaborately beaded blue cape of the same design as the others. Without a word of hesitation, he placed the cape around her shoulders, and said: "This is the cape of service." Then he seated himself in the chair and said to Mona: "Come and take a picture with me!" Mona was breathless with astonishment at the bounties being showered on her and could hardly walk. She looked up and saw a man sitting behind an old-fashioned camera covered by a cloth. Bahá'u'lláh repeated his instruction but Mona could not move. Then Bahá'u'lláh took her arm, saying, "Mehdi, take our picture." And he took a picture of them together. The flash of the camera wakened her abruptly and she pleaded tearfully to be able to finish her dream and then fell asleep again. Bahá'u'lláh had left the room. Only the photographer remained, carrying the tripod and camera on his shoulder as if to leave. He turned around and asked Mona to convey his love to his children. But Mona could not tell which "Mehdi" he was since there were many people by that name in the long history of the Faith and in her own community. But still he looked familiar to her. "Mehdi" was busily tying his shoes and noticed that Mona did not recognize him. As he was leaving the room he turned and said, "I am Medhi Anvari." Mona instantly recognized him as one of the Bahá'ís of <u>Sh</u>íráz who had previously been killed.[121]

# 122

One day, which coincided with a Bahá'í Holy Day, Mona wanted to say prayers alone instead of joining a small prayer session organized by the Bahá'í prisoners. Mona, in fact, had been spending increasing amounts of time alone. Often, when the other prisoners would congregate together, Mona would find an empty cell to pray and meditate by herself. On this occasion, however, her mother insisted that Mona join them, so she acquiesced. Later in the day, she took her mother aside and said, "Mother, I would have wanted very much to spend this last holy day alone, to pray and meditate on my own." Mona's mother didn't understand what she meant and said, "If you had told me, I wouldn't have minded. Why did you agree so quickly?" Mona said, "Because you have the right to ask me to be with you." Mona then took her aside and said, "Mother, I want to tell you something, please come with me." She led her mother down a corridor that was so narrow that they had to walk in single file. Suddenly Mona stopped, turned around, and said, "Mother, do you know that they are going to execute me?" Her mother became very upset and refused to listen. She was completely unaware of the spiritual state that Mona had reached and said, "No, dear, you'll be free, released from the prison. You will have a family and children. I want to see your children. Please don't think this way." Mona became upset and said, "I swear to God that I do not wish this for myself and you shouldn't wish it for me. I know that they are going to kill me and I want to tell you what I am going to do when that happens. If you don't let me tell you now, you will regret it in the future. Now, do you want to let me tell you or not?" Mona's mother was stunned and said, "Yes, tell me." Then Mona faced her and said, "You know Mother, at the place where they're going to take us for our execution, we will have to go up and stand on something high where they will put a rope around our necks . . . Then I'm going to kiss [the] noose and say a prayer." Mona then folded her arms across her chest, closed her eyes and with a blissful look on her face said a short prayer. Then she opened her eyes and said, "I'll say that prayer for the happiness and prosperity of all mankind and bid farewell to this mortal world and go to God." Then she looked at her mother, who was staring at her in a state of confusion and bewilderment. All she could say was, "That was a nice story, Mona." Mona's eyes filled with tears. Quietly, she said, "Mother, it was not a story. Why won't you believe me?"

Two days later, Mona and the other nine women were told that they would be given one more chance to recant their Faith or be sentenced to die. It was their last chance to remain alive. That night, Mona had another dream in which she was in prison saying the long obligatory prayer. 'Abdu'l-Bahá came through the cell door and sat on the bed on which Mona's mother was sleeping. Ṭáhirih Siyavushi was sleeping on the floor. He patted her mother's head and raised His other hand towards Mona, who thought to herself that He might leave if she continued saying her prayer. So she sat on her knees in front of 'Abdu'l-Bahá and held her hands in His. 'Abdu'l-Bahá asked Mona, "What do you want?" Mona replied, "Steadfastness." 'Abdu'l-Bahá asked again, "What do you want from us?" Mona replied, "Steadfastness for all the friends." 'Abdu'l-Bahá asked for a third time, "What do you want?" Mona again replied, "Steadfastness." Then 'Abdu'l-Bahá said twice, "It is granted. It is granted."[122]

# 123

Luda, a highly educated Russian lady with two degrees in Space Technology and Finance, found the Bahá'í Faith in 2009. Here is her story:

Luda has lived in America—in Nashua, New Hampshire—for about three years. She has a Russian friend who resides in California, whom she came to know over the internet through a tax consultant service. In August of 2009, this friend sent her a precious prayer, telling Luda that this prayer had helped her through a difficult time. The California friend is a member of the Bahá'í Faith. The prayer, which is called the *Tablet of Aḥmad*, was in English. Since Luda's English is not as strong as her Russian, she decided to look for the Russian translation of this tablet on the Internet. The words of this prayer, Luda says, were so beautiful and moving that she felt a compelling power to investigate the source. To her surprise it was from the sacred writings of the Bahá'í Faith. She describes the Bahá'í writings as words for the heart and soul, easy to understand, unlike reading the Latin words that she grew up reading in her Christian upbringing in Russia and could not understand. Looking at more and more of the Bahá'í writings started to attract her heart with incredible curiosity about the truth of this new religion. Coming from an Orthodox Christian background, she was a bit hesitant at the beginning, guilty and afraid to seek other truths, so she prayed to God every day to show her a sign of this truth.

Her wish was granted in many ways. A few days later, Luda saw her deceased mother in an unusual dream. In that dream, her mother told her that she must go to Moscow soon. Luda asked her mother (who had died five years earlier) why she hadn't come in her dreams before; why now and why should she go to Moscow? But her mother insisted that she go to Russia. Luda found the idea of traveling intriguing, but did not have the money to buy a ticket. A humorous event happened while she was with her husband on a weekend trip to a casino in Connecticut. Luda prayed and prayed to God to win money and at the last minute of their visit she did win $1,500; the exact amount she needed for a ticket to Moscow! Luda told her Bahá'í friend in California of her interest in the new religion and her friend connected Luda with Bahá'ís residing in the same city in New Hampshire where Luda lives. When contacted by the Bahá'ís of Nashua, Luda told them she was on her way to Russia the very next day. They encouraged her to seek out the Bahá'ís in Moscow and she assured them that she intended to do so. As soon as she arrived in Russia, she looked online for information about the Bahá'í Faith there. Immediately she was taken into the arms of that community, where she felt tremendous love and spent her time reading and investigating the truth.

On December 31, Luda had another significant dream, this time she saw a holy figure with a white turban and a white beard, later on she suspected it was 'Abdu'l-Bahá, the son of the Founder of the Bahá'í Faith. In the dream, he lovingly told her that she must never pray to God about money. When she woke up, she felt tremendous joy and spirituality, and decided at that moment that she believed in this religion and that she was a Bahá'í.

Luda's trip to Russia lasted much longer than anticipated, as she decided to introduce her new business of scrapbooking to Russia. This has proven very successful. She returned to New Hampshire in July of 2010, and informed the local Bahá'ís that she had accepted the Bahá'í Faith in Russia and was eager to join her new community in Nashua, where she has been warmly welcomed.

Luda continues to have spiritual dreams of utmost happiness and love. Her life has changed for the better in so many ways; even her husband noticed her new happiness and energy. She is delighted to have found this amazing faith and says she feels the true meaning of love towards all mankind.[123]

# NOTES

**Introduction**

1. 'Abdu'l-Bahá, *Memorials of the Faithful,* pp. 190–91.
2. The Qur'án, 12:3.
3. Bahá'u'lláh, *Gleanings from the Writings of Bahá'u'lláh,* no. 39.1.
4. The Báb, quoted in Nabíl-i-A'zam, *The Dawn-Breakers,* p. 61.
5. Bahá'u'lláh, quoted in Shoghi Effendi, *God Passes By,* p. 36.
6. Shoghi Effendi, *God Passes By,* pp. 36–37.
7. Bahá'u'lláh, *The Seven Valleys,* p. 59.
8. The Qur'án, 12:22.
9. Ibid., 12:101.
10. Ibid., 12:4.
11. Ibid., 12:100.
12. Saeidi, *Gate of the Heart,* p. 148.
13. Bulkeley, "Transforming Dreams, Dream Time," *Magazine of the Association for the Study of Dreams,* issue 02/18/2011.
14. Job 33:14–16.
15. Shoghi Effendi, *God Passes By,* p. 143.
16. Bahá'u'lláh, *Tablets of Bahá'u'lláh,* p. 187.
17. 'Abdu'l-Bahá, *The Promulgation of Universal Peace,* p. 416.
18. Mázindarání, *Amr va Khalq,* 1:323.
19. Byron, *The Works of Lord Byron,* p. 32.
20. Lewis, *The Dream Encyclopedia: Religion and Dreams.* http://books.google.com/.
21. Bahá'u'lláh, *Tablets of Bahá'u'lláh,* pp. 187–88.
22. Bahá'u'lláh, *The Seven Valleys,* p. 34.

23. 'Abdu'l-Bahá, *Promulgation of Universal Peace*, p. 586.
24. Mázindarání, *Amr va Khalq*, 1:326–27.
25. Ibid., 1:322.
26. From a letter written on behalf of Shoghi Effendi, in Helen Hornby, *Lights of Guidance*, p. 513.
27. Shoghi Effendi, *God Passes By*, p. 162.

**Dreams of Destiny**
1. Translated and adapted from Muhammad-'Alí Faizi, *Hadrat-i Nuqtay-i-Ula, The Life Of the Báb*, pp. 7–8.
2. Ibid., p. 19.
3. A. L. M. Nicolas, quoted in Nabíl-i-A'zam, *The Dawn-Breakers*, p. 1, note 3.
4. Nabíl-i-A'zam, *The Dawn-Breakers*, p. 9, note 3.
5. Ibid., pp. 42–45.
6. Afnan, "The Bab in Shiraz: An Account by Mirza Habibu'llah Afnan," *Bahá'í Studies Review* 12 (2004): 15.
7. Balyuzi, *Khadíjih Bagum: Wife of the Báb*, p. 2.
8. Balyuzi, *Bahá'u'lláh: The King of Glory*, p. 346.
9. Nabíl-i-A'zam, *The Dawn-Breakers*, p. 253.
10. Translated and adapted from Muhammad-Husaini, *The Báb*, p. 777.
11. Translated and adapted from Mázindarání, *Amr va Khalq*, 1:322–23.
12. Translated and adapted from Goharriz, *Letters of the Living*, p. 80.
13. Nabíl-i-A'zam, *The Dawn-Breakers*, p. 82.
14. 'Abdu'l-Bahá, *Memorials of the Faithful*, pp. 192–93.
15. Nabíl-i-A'zam, *The Dawn-Breakers*, pp. 87–88.
16. Balyuzi, *Khadíjih Bagum: The Wife of the Bab*, p. 5.
17. Nabíl-i-A'zam, *The Dawn-Breakers*, pp. 191–92.
18. Sears, *Release the Sun*, pp. 57–60.
19. Nabíl-i-A'zam, *The Dawn-Breakers*, pp. 217–18.
20. Ibid., pp. 255–56.
21. Ibid., pp. 303–5.
22. Ibid., pp. 303, 70.
23. Ibid., pp. 344–45.
24. Ibid., p. 405.
25. Translated and adapted from Muhammad-Husaini, pp. 481–84.
26. Adapted from Anwar Smith, *Munírih Khanum, Memoirs and Letters*, p. 5.
27. Anwar Smith, *Munírih Khanum, Memoirs and Letters*, p. 15.
28. Blomfield, *The Chosen Highway*, p. 194.
29. Nabíl-i-A'zam, *The Dawn-Breakers*, pp. 119–120.
30. Balyuzi, *Bahá'u'lláh: The King of Glory*, p. 19.
31. Ibid., p. 21.

32. Ibid., pp. 21–22.
33. Bahá'u'lláh, *Epistle to the Son of the Wolf*, p. 21.
34. Nabíl-i-A'ẓam, *The Dawn-Breakers*, pp. 633–34.
35. Balyuzi, *Bahá'u'lláh: The King of Glory*, p. 109.
36. Translated and adopted from Afnán, *Ahd-i A'la, Zindganiy-i Hadrat-i Báb*, p. 506.
37. Badiei, *Stories Told by 'Abdu'l-Bahá*, p. 92.
38. Shoghi Effendi, *God Passes By*, p. 231.
39. From Lawh-i Tabib, provisional translation, *M'aidih-yi Asmani*, edited by 'Abdu'l-Hamid Ishraq-khavari, 8:78.
40. Ali-Akbar Furutan, *Stories of Bahá'u'lláh*, #24.
41. Balyuzi, *Bahá'u'lláh: The King of Glory*, p. 198.
42. Nabíl-i-A'ẓam, quoted in ibid., p. 266.
43. Taherzadeh, *The Revelation of Bahá'u'lláh*, 3:5–7.
44. Ibid., 2:197–99.
45. Ibid., 4:53.
46. Ibid., 3:65–67.
47. Ibid., 3:168–70.
48. Ibid., 2:129–35.
49. Anwar Smith, *Munírih, Memoirs and Letters*, p. 21.
50. Ibid., pp. 24–25.
51. Ibid., pp. 38–46.
52. Translated and adapted from *Bihjatu's-sudur*, p. 266.
53. Balyuzi, *Eminent Bahá'ís in the Time of Bahá'u'lláh*, pp. 40–41.
54. Taherzadeh, *The Revelation of Bahá'u'lláh* 4:223–25.
55. Translated and adapted from Ishraq-khavari, *Muhadirat*, pp. 319–21.
56. Translated and adapted from 'Azizu'llah Sulaymani, *Masabih-i Hidayat, Lamps of Guidance* 2:92–106.
57. Ibid., 2:106–8.
58. Ibid., 4:386.
59. Ibid., 1:139–40.
60. Faizi, *Fire on the Mountaintop*, p. 23.
61. Translated and adapted from 'Azizu'llah Sulaymani, *Masabih-i Hidayat, Lamps of Guidance*, 1:106–32.
62. Ibid.
63. Taherzadeh, *The Revelation of Bahá'u'lláh*, 4:185.
64. Stockman, *The Bahá'í Faith in America: Origins, 1892–1900* 1:141.
65. Translated and adapted from Riaz Ghadimi, *Sultán-i Rosol, King of the Messengers*, pp. 35–36.
66. Stockman, *The Bahá'í Faith in America: Origins, 1892–1900*, 15.
67. Ibid.

68. Mr. Brent Poirier, Internet posting and personal correspondence.
69. Badiei, *Stories told by 'Abdu'l-Bahá*, p. 129.
70. Abu'l-Qasim Faizi, *Da'stan-i Doostan*, p. 24.
71. 'Abdu'l-Bahá, *Memorials of the Faithful*, pp. 10–12.
72. Balyuzi, *'Abdu'l-Bahá: The Centre of the Covenant*, p. 119.
73. Ruḥiyyih Khánum, *The Priceless Pearl*, pp. 10, 16.
74. Translated and adapted from 'Azizu'llah Sulaymani, *Masabih-i Hidayat, Lights of Guidance*, 3:247–52.
75. Afroukhteh, *Memories of Nine Years in 'Akká*, pp. 367–68.
76. Ibid., pp. 347–48.
77. Thompson, *The Diary of Juliet Thompson*, p. 179.
78. Ibid., p. 89.
79. Ibid., p. 104.
80. Ibid., pp. 185–86.
81. Ibid., pp. 204–5.
82. Ibid., p. 234.
83. Translated and adapted from Zarqani, *Badayi'u-l Athar*, 2:290.
84. Blomfield, *The Chosen Highway*, p. 185.
85. Adapted from *Star of the West*, 9:9:102.
86. Lacroix-Hopson, *'Abdu'l-Bahá in New York*, p. 44.
87. Garst, *'Abdu'l-Bahá, The Most Mighty Branch*, p. 169.
88. Adapted from *Star of the West*, 14:12:365–67.
89. Blomfield, *The Chosen Highway*, p. 215.
90. Rohani, *Sweet and enchanting stories*, p. 119.
91. Reflections on the Bahá'í Faith, http://bahai-insights.blogspot.com/2010/05/bahaullahs-twigs-and-stones.html.
92. Translated and adapted from 'Azizu'llah Sulaymani, *Masabih-i Hidayat, Lamps of Guidance*, 6:311–12.
93. Translated and adapted from Amanat, *Bahá'íyan-e Kashan*, pp. 210–11.
94. Lady Blomfield, *The Chosen Highway*, p. 216.
95. 'Abdu'l-Bahá, quoted in Shoghi Effendi, *God Passes By*, p. 491.
96. Lady Blomfield and Shoghi Effendi, *Bahá'í World* 1:19.
97. Translated and adapted from *Risalih-i Ayyam-i Tesa'*, p. 495.
98. Munje, *The Reincarnation Mystery Revealed*, pp. 91–93.
99. *Bahá'í World*, 12:710.
100. Concerning this dream, Mr. Poirier wrote to the author of this book, "Hi Amir. To my knowledge the story is not published anywhere. I can, however, verify the authenticity of the story because of two things. First, I heard it from Inez herself, talking about her sister's vision. Second, Inez had a postcard from the woman who received the flowers and the money, and I have a copy of it somewhere in my papers. In it the woman says that she never dreamed of so great a gift from God, and at such a low time in her life."

101. Harper, *Lights of Fortitude*, p. 138.
102. *Bahá'í World*, 7:786.
103. Faizi, *Milly*, p. 6.
104. Translated and adapted from Khoshbin-Samandari, *Taraz-i Samandari*, 1:31.
105. Adapted from the article by Agnes B. Alexander, *Star of the West* 22:9:276–77.
106. Alexander, *History of the Bahá'í Faith in Japan.*
107. Adapted from Furutan, *The Story of my Heart*, pp. 1–3.
108. Ibid., pp. 51–52.
109. Nakhjavani, *The Great African Safari*, p. 52.
110. Ibid., p. 287.
111. Ibid., p. 338.
112. Rúhíyyih Khánum, *The Priceless Pearl*, p. 143.
113. Gilstrap, *From Copper To Gold*, pp. 302–3.
114. Sears, *Hands of the Cause, Bill*, p. 8.
115. Khadem, *The Vision of Shoghi Effendi, Service at the Threshold*, p. 105
116. Rabbani, *Hands of the Cause, Enoch Olinga*, p. 11.
117. Muhajir, *Hand of the Cause*, pp. 353–54.
118. Ibid., p. 643.
119. Dr. David Young's e-mail of 12-16-11.
120. Translated and adapted from *Payam-i Bahá'í*, issue no. 186.
121. *The Story of Mona*, http://www.adressformona.org/monasstory/storyofmona4.htm.
122. Ibid.
123. *Liudmila St. Onge (Luda): Why Bahá'í?* http://www.bahai.us/2010/11/04/why-bahai-liudmila-st-onge-luda/.

# BIBLIOGRAPHY

**Works by Bahá'u'lláh**

*Epistle to the Son of the Wolf.* Wilmette, IL: Bahá'í Publishing Trust, 1988.

*Gleanings from the Writings of Bahá'u'lláh.* Wilmette, IL: Bahá'í Publishing, 2005.

*The Seven Valleys and the Four Valleys.* Wilmette, IL: Bahá'í Publishing Trust, 1991.

*Tablets of Bahá'u'lláh revealed after the Kitáb-i-Aqdas.* Compiled by the Research Department of the Universal House of Justice. Wilmette, IL: Bahá'í Publishing Trust, 1988.

**Works by 'Abdu'l-Bahá**

*Memorials of the Faithful.* Wilmette, IL: Bahá'í Publishing Trust, 1971.

*The Promulgation of Universal Peace: Talks Delivered by 'Abdu'l-Bahá during His Visit to the United States and Canada in 1912.* Wilmette, IL: Bahá'í Publishing Trust, 2007.

**Works by Shoghi Effendi**

*God Passes By.* Wilmette, IL: Bahá'í Publishing Trust, 1974.

**Other Titles**

Afnán, Abu'l-Qásim. *'Ahd-i A'lá; Zindegáníy-i Hadrat-i Báb.* Oxford: Oneworld Publications. 2000.

Afnán, Mírzá Habíb. *Memories of the Báb, Bahá'u'lláh and 'Abdu'l-Bahá.* Los Angeles: Kalimat Press, 2005.

———. *The Bab in Shiraz.* Translated by Ahang Rabbani. *Bahá'í Studies Review* 12 (2004): 15. http://bahai-library.com/pdf/r/rabbani_habibullah_afnan_shiraz.pdf

Afrou<u>kh</u>teh, Yuness. *Memories of Nine Years in 'Akká*. Translated by Riaz Masrour. Oxford: George Ronald, 2003.

Alexander, Agnes Baldwin. *History of the Baha'i Faith in Hawaii*. Osaka: Japan Bahá'í Publishing Trust, 1977.

Amanat, Mousa. *Baha'iyan-e Kashan*. Madrid: Fundacion Nehal, 2012.

Anwar Smith, Sammireh. *Munirih Khanum, Memoirs and Letters*. Los Angeles, CA: Kalimat Press, 1986.

Badiei, Amir. *Stories Told by 'Abdu'l-Bahá*. Oxford: George Ronald, 2003.

*Bahá'í World*, Vols. 7 and 12. Wilmette, IL: Bahá'í Publishing, 1939 and 1956, respectively.

———. Vol. 18. Oxford: University Press, 1986.

Balyuzi, H. M. *Bahá'u'lláh: The King of Glory*. Oxford: George Ronald, 1991.

———. *'Abdu'l-Bahá: The Centre of the Covenant of Bahá'u'lláh*. London: George Ronald, 1971.

———. *Khadijih Bagum: The Wife of the Báb*. Oxford: George Ronald, 1981.

———. *Eminent Bahá'ís in the Time of Bahá'u'lláh*. Southampton: The Camelot Press, 1985.

Blomfield, Lady (Sitarih Khanum). *The Chosen Highway*. Wilmette, IL: Bahá'í Publishing Trust, 1956.

Bulkeley, Kelly. *Transforming Dreams*. Dream Time Magazine, Issue 02/18/2011.

Byron, George Gordon. *The Works of Lord Byron*. http://archive.org/stream/theworksoflordby20158gut/20158-0.txt

Chapman, Anita Ios. *Leroy Ioas, Hand of the Cause of God*. http://bahai-insights.blogspot.com/2010/05/bahaullahs-twigs-and-stones.html.

Faizi, Abu'l-Qasim. *Dástan-i Doostan*. Tihrán: Bahá'i Publishing Trust, 1967.

———. *Milly*. Oxford: George Ronald, 1977.

Faizi, Gloria. *Fire on the Mountaintop*. London: The Bahá'í Publishing Trust, 1973.

Faizi, Muhammad-Ali. *Hadrat-i Nuqtay-i-Ula, The Life Of The Báb*. Hofheim-Langenhain: Bahá'í-Verlag, 1987.

Fath-i A'zam, Shafiqeh. *Kháb-i Ajeeb: Strange Dream*. Paris: Payam-i Bahá'í #186 (magazine), 1995.

Freeman Gilstrap, Dorothy. *From Copper to Gold*. Oxford: George Ronald, 1984.

Furutan, 'Ali-Akbar. *Stories of Bahá'u'lláh*. Oxford: George Ronald, 1986.

———. *The Story of My Heart*. Oxford: George Ronald, 1977.

Garst, Hitjo. *The Most Mighty Branch*. Oxford: George Ronald, 2007.

Ghadimi, Riaz. *King of the Messengers, the Bab*. Toronto: Univ. of Toronto Press, 1987.

Goharriz, Hooshang. *Letters of the Living*. Phoenix, AZ: Badi Publishing, 2004.

Ḥájí Mírzá Haydar-'Alí. *Bihjatu's-Sudur*. Bombay: 1913.

Harper, Barron. *Lights of Fortitude*. Oxford: George Ronald, 1997.

Hornby, Helen. *Lights of Guidance: A Bahá'í Reference File*. New Delhi: Bahá'í Publishing Trust, 1988.

Ishraq-Khavari, Abdu'l-Hamid. *Ayyam-i Tesa'.* Tihran: Bahá'í Publishing Trust, 1947.
———. *Ma'idih-'i Asmani.* Vol. 8. Tihran Bahá'í Publishing Trust, 1972.
———. *Muhádirát.* Hofheim-Langenhain: Bahá'í-Verlag, 1987.
Khadem, Dhikru'llah. *The Vision of Shoghi Effendi, Service at the Threshold.* Ocean Bahá'í Library.
Khoshbin-Samandari, Parivash. *Taraz-i Samandari.* Ontario: Institute for Bahá'í Studies in Persian, 2002.
Lacroix-Hopson, Elaine. *'Abdu'l-Bahá in New York: The City of the Covenant.* New York: NewVistaDesign, 1999.
Lewis, R. James, *Dream Encyclopedia.* http://books.google.com/.
Mázindaráni, Fádil. *Amr va Khalq.* Vol. Hofheim-Langenhain: Bahá'í-Verlag, 1985.
Muhajir, Iran Furutan. *Dr Muhajir: Hand of the Cause of God.* London: The Bahá'í Publishing Trust, 1992.
Muhammad-Husaini, Nusrat'u'llah. *The Báb.* Ontario, Canada: Institute for Bahá'í Studies in Persian, 1995.
Munje, H. M. *The Reincarnation Mystery Revealed.* New Delhi: Bahá'í Publishing Trust, 1997.
Nabíl-i-A'zam. [Muhammad-i-Zarandí]. *The Dawn-Breakers: Nabíl's Narrative of the Early Days of the Bahá'í Revelation.* Translated and edited by Shoghi Effendi. Wilmette, IL: Bahá'í Publishing Trust, 1962.
Nakhjavani, Violette. *The Great African Safari.* Oxford: Goeorge Ronald, 2002.
*New King James Version.* http://www.biblegateway.com/versions/New-King-James-Version-NKJV-Bible.
Poirier, Brent. *A Covenant Unique in the Spiritual Annals of Mankind.* Posted in 2009. http://bahai-covenant.blogspot.com.
Rabbani, Ruhiyyih. *The Priceless Pearl.* London: Bahá'i Publishing Trust, 1969
———. *Hands of the Cause, Enoch Olinga.* Nairobi: Bahá'í Publishing Agency, 2001.
Rohani, Aziz. *Sweet and Enchanting Stories.* Mustang, OK: Juxta Publishing Limited, 2005.
Saiedi, Nader, *Gate of the Heart.* Waterloo, Ont.: Wilfrid Laurier Press, 2008.
Sears, Marguerite Reimer. *Hands of the Cause, Bill.* Eloy, Arizona: Desert Rose Bahá'í Institute, Inc., 2003.
Sears, William. *Release the Sun.* Wilmette, IL: Bahá'í Publishing Trust, 2003.
*Star of the West.* Chicago: Bahá'í News Service, 1918, 1924, and 1931.
Stockman, Robert. *The Bahá'í Faith in America: Origins, 1892–1900.* Wilmette, IL: Bahá'í Publishing, 1985.
Sulaymáni, 'Azizu'llah. *Masábih-i Hedáyat (Lamps of Guidance).* Vols. 1–6. Tihrán: Bahá'i Publishing Trust, 1948–1969.
Taherzadeh, Adib. *The Revelation of Bahá'u'lláh.* 4 vols. Oxford: George Ronald, 1983.
*The Ministry of the Custodians,* 1957–1963. Haifa: Bahá'í World Centre, 1992.

Thompson, Juliet. *The Diary of Julet Thompson*. Los Angeles: Kalimat Press, 1983.

Yusuf Ali, A., trans. *The Qur'án*. London: The Islamic Foundation, 1975.

Zarqani, Mahmud. *Badayi'u-l Athar*, vol. 2. Hofheim-Langenhain: Bahá'í-Verlag, 1982.

## Bahá'í PUBLISHING

## Bahá'í Publishing and the Bahá'í Faith

Bahá'í Publishing produces books based on the teachings of the Bahá'í Faith. Founded over 160 years ago, the Bahá'í Faith has spread to some 235 nations and territories and is now accepted by more than five million people. The word "Bahá'í" means "follower of Bahá'u'lláh." Bahá'u'lláh, the founder of the Bahá'í Faith, asserted that He is the Messenger of God for all of humanity in this day. The cornerstone of His teachings is the establishment of the spiritual unity of humankind, which will be achieved by personal transformation and the application of clearly identified spiritual principles. Bahá'ís also believe that there is but one religion and that all the Messengers of God—among them Abraham, Zoroaster, Moses, Krishna, Buddha, Jesus, and Muḥammad—have progressively revealed its nature. Together, the world's great religions are expressions of a single, unfolding divine plan. Human beings, not God's Messengers, are the source of religious divisions, prejudices, and hatreds.

The Bahá'í Faith is not a sect or denomination of another religion, nor is it a cult or a social movement. Rather, it is a globally recognized independent world religion founded on new books of scripture revealed by Bahá'u'lláh.

Bahá'í Publishing is an imprint of the National Spiritual Assembly of the Bahá'ís of the United States.

For more information about the Bahá'í Faith,
or to contact Bahá'ís near you,
visit http://www.bahai.us/
or call
1-800-22-UNITE

# Other Books Available from Bahá'í Publishing

**BLESSED IS THE SPOT**
Bahá'u'lláh
Illustrated by Constance von Kitzing
$12.00 US / $14.00 CAN
Paper Over Board
ISBN 978-1-61851-048-8

*A beautifully illustrated prayer book for children; a perfect book for the whole family to treasure.*

*Blessed is the Spot* is a simple and beautiful prayer book for children. Illustrated with warm and inviting imagery by Constanze von Kitzing, whose work strikes the perfect balance between playful and reverent, the book contains a single prayer from the writings of the Bahá'í Faith. The prayer has long been loved and cherished by the Bahá'í community for its exquisite yet accessible words, and it is hoped that many new readers, both children and parents alike, will fall in love with it and find inspiration in its uplifting words.

**ONE REALITY**
THE HARMONY OF SCIENCE AND RELIGION
Compiled by Bonnie J. Taylor
$16.00 US / $18.00 CAN
Trade Paper
ISBN 978-1-61851-049-5

*A unique compilation that demonstrates the harmony of science and religion, and explores how both can assist in understanding the world around us.*

*One Reality: The Harmony of Science and Religion* is a compilation of passages from the Bahá'í writings that explores the relationship between science and religion, and demonstrates the Bahá'í perspective that the two seemingly opposing forces can exist in perfect harmony. As 'Abdu'l-Bahá, the son of the Prophet and Founder of the Bahá'í Faith, states: "If we say religion is opposed to science, we lack knowledge of either true science or true religion, for both are founded upon the premises and conclusions of reason, and both must bear its test." Meticulously researched and compiled by Bonnie J. Taylor, *One Reality* offers a comprehensive overview of the subject from a Bahá'í perspective, and includes a thought-provoking and challenging introduction from John S. Hatcher, a highly respected academic and the author of numerous books about Bahá'í scripture and theology.

**SPIRIT OF FAITH**

Life After Death

Bahá'í Publishing

$12.00 US / $14.00 CAN

Hardcover

ISBN 978-1-61851-047-1

*The seventh book in the Spirit of Faith series focuses on the subject of life after death and the immortality of the human soul.*

*Spirit of Faith: Life After Death* is a compilation of writings and prayers that explore the topic of death and the transition from this life to the worlds beyond our world. Many of the writings of the Bahá'í Faith emphasize our limited time on this planet and the importance of our conduct while here. The passages compiled here touch on the immortality of the human soul, the importance of detachment from earthly desires, and the continuation of life in the spiritual worlds of God. Similar to previous titles in this series, this collection of sacred scripture can help define our place within a single, unfolding, divine creation. The *Spirit of Faith* series continues to explore spiritual topics—such as the unity of humanity, the eternal covenant of God, the promise of world peace, and more—by presenting what the central figures of the Bahá'í Faith have written regarding these important topics.

**WAVE WATCHER**
Craig Alan Johnson
$14.00 US / $16.00 CAN
Trade Paper
ISBN 978-1-61851-046-4

*A thoughtful and beautifully written young-adult novel about a young boy growing up and dealing with a tragic event that shapes his life and understanding of the world.*

Twelve-year-old Ray can't sleep. Everyone thinks it's because of bad dreams, but it's not. His thoughts keep him awake—especially tonight, exactly one year after the devastating event that changed his life forever. The gifted young writer's pen has been silent since then, stilled by the shock. Tonight Ray will break the silence. He will begin to write again. Looking back on his short life, he will tell the story of who he is and try to make sense of the patterns that once seemed so sure. In the process he will come to see how a broken-down house, a brother with only one lung, the Mozart his mother plays on the piano, his father's novel, a whisper in a cave, a grandmother who prays at midnight, and a man-eating Chihuahua have helped him make sense of the patterns in his life. *Wave Watcher* is a story about what it means to be an everyday hero, and what it means to be human. Author Craig Johnson's novel, written for a young adult audience, will make us laugh, cry, hope, and strive to live as fully as possible.